Introduction

This Companion is a source of reference for users of mathematics and statistics: students in a variety of subjects, including mathematics, at AS and A level, in Higher Education and on many vocational courses, and those who use mathematics in their everyday lives and at work. It contains a large number of formulae, explanations of the meanings of terms, statistical tables and other useful information.

The origins of this book lie in the *Students' Handbook,* first published in 1992 for AS and A level students taking modules in the MEI Structured Mathematics scheme. In the following years, this book went through a number of editions, each containing more information and more helpfully laid out. In 2006 MEI and Hodder Murray decided to publish a completely new version that would benefit a much larger clientele, and so it now covers all the A level specifications in mathematics and much more.

If you are taking an examination in mathematics or statistics, you may be expected to know certain formulae and to get others in a formula book for use in the examination; check this with your teacher or your examination specification. Although there is a lot of information in this booklet, it is not a definitive list of what you need to know for your examination. Whatever your level of study, you will almost certainly also need formulae from earlier levels.

To help you find your way round this Companion, there is a contents list and index.

The original *Students' Handbook* was largely the work of Roger Porkess. The whole MEI team have contributed to its transformation into this Companion but by far the majority of the work has been done by Stella Dudzic. Thanks are due to Michael Davies (Westminster School) and Nigel Green (Denstone College) who computed some of the statistical tables. We sincerely hope that you will find it useful, not just when you are a student but also to keep on your shelf and continue to refer to for years to come.

Code letter	Where you are most likely to first encounter the formulae
A	GCSE or AS Mathematics core module
B	A level Mathematics core module
C	AS or A level optional module
D	Further Mathematics A level
E	Further Mathematics A level or beyond

The Publishers would like to thank the following for permission to reproduce copyright material:

Acknowledgements
The tables on pages 65, 70, 71, 72 and 73 are reproduced from *Elementary Statistics Tables*, H.R. Neave, © 1981 by permission of Taylor & Francis Books UK.
The tables on pages 68 and 69 are based on tables produced by K. Pearson in Biometrika reproduced by permission of Oxford University Press with additional values as given in Cambridge Elementary Statistical Tables by D.V. Lindley and J.C.P. Miller, © 1963 published and reproduced by permission of Cambridge University Press.
Every effort has been made to trace all copyright holders, but if any have been inadvertently overlooked the Publishers will be pleased to make the necessary arrangements at the first opportunity.

Hodder Headline's policy is to use papers that are natural, renewable and recyclable products and made from wood grown in sustainable forests. The logging and manufacturing processes are expected to conform to the environmental regulations of the country of origin.

Orders: please contact Bookpoint Ltd, 130 Milton Park, Abingdon, Oxon OX14 4SB. Telephone: (44) 01235 827720. Fax: (44) 01235 400454. Lines are open 9.00 – 5.00, Monday to Saturday, with a 24-hour message answering service. Visit our website at www.hoddereducation.co.uk

© MEI 2007
First published in 2007 by
Hodder Murray, an imprint of Hodder Education,
an Hachette Livre UK company,
338 Euston Road
London NW1 3BH

Impression number   5 4 3 2 1
Year   2012 2011 2010 2009 2008 2007

Typeset in 10pt Times New Roman by Pantek Arts Ltd, Maidstone, Kent.
Printed in Spain

A catalogue record for this title is available from the British Library

ISBN-13: 978 0 340 95923 7

Contents

Units, constants, areas and volumes and Greek letters

SI units and their prefixes

SI units are based on metres, kilograms and seconds; there is more on SI units on page 34.

yotta (Y)	10^{24}
zetta (Z)	10^{21}
exa (E)	10^{18}
peta (P)	10^{15}
tera (T)	10^{12}
giga (G)	10^{9}
mega (M)	10^{6}
kilo (k)	10^{3}
hecto (h)	10^{2}
deca (da)	10
deci (d)	10^{-1}
centi (c)	10^{-2}
milli (m)	10^{-3}
micro (μ)	10^{-6}
nano (n)	10^{-9}
pico (p)	10^{-12}
femto (f)	10^{-15}
atto (a)	10^{-18}
zepto (z)	10^{-21}
yocto (y)	10^{-24}

Conversion between metric units

1 hectare = $10000\,\text{m}^2$
1 litre = $1000\,\text{cm}^3$

1 tonne = 1000 kg
$1\,\text{m}\,\text{s}^{-1} = 3.6\,\text{km}\,\text{hr}^{-1}$

Conversion between imperial and metric units

1 yard $\approx$ 0.914 m
1 mile $\approx$ 1.609 km
1 mph $\approx 0.447\,\text{m}\,\text{s}^{-1}$
1 pint $\approx$ 0.568 litres
1 gallon $\approx$ 4.546 litres

$1\,\text{m} \approx 3\,\text{ft}\ 3.4\,\text{in}$
1 km $\approx$ 0.621 miles
$1\,\text{m}\,\text{s}^{-1} \approx 2.24\,\text{mph}$
1 litre $\approx$ 1.760 pints
1 litre $\approx$ 0.220 gallons
1 kg $\approx$ 2.205 lb

1 lb $\approx$ 0.454 kg
1 ton $\approx$ 1.016 tonnes
1 acre $\approx$ 0.405 hectares

1 tonne $\approx$ 0.984 tons
1 hectare $\approx$ 2.471 acres

Earth measurements

Earth's equatorial radius	6378.135 km
Earth's polar radius	6356.750 km
Mean distance of earth from sun	1.496×10^{8} km
Mean distance of moon from earth	384400 km
Mass of the earth	5.976×10^{24} kg
Mass of the moon	7.349×10^{22} kg
Mass of the sun	1.98892×10^{30} kg

Physical constants

$g = 9.80665\,\text{m}\,\text{s}^{-2}$ Standard acceleration due to gravity
(The acceleration due to gravity varies over the surface of the earth; this standard value is the average value at sea level at a latitude of 45.5°.)
$G \approx 6.67 \times 10^{-11}\,\text{N}\,\text{m}^2\,\text{kg}^{-2}$ Gravitational constant
$c = 299792458\,\text{m}\,\text{s}^{-1}$ Speed of light *in vacuo*

Mathematical constants

$\pi = 3.14159\ldots$	Ratio of circumference to diameter of a circle
$e = 2.71828\ldots$	Base of natural logarithms
$\gamma = 0.57721\ldots$	Euler's constant: $\lim\limits_{n \to \infty}\left(\sum\limits_{r=1}^{n}\frac{1}{r} - \ln n\right)$
$\delta = 4.66920\ldots$	Feigenbaum's constant (sometimes the symbol σ is used)

Area and volume

Area of a trapezium $= \frac{1}{2}(a+b)h$
Area of a circle $= \pi r^2$
Volume of a prism = cross-sectional area $\times$ length
Volume of a cylinder $= \pi r^2 h$
Volume of a sphere $= \frac{4}{3}\pi r^3$
Surface area of a sphere $= 4\pi r^2$
Volume of a pyramid or cone $= \frac{1}{3} \times$ base area $\times$ height
Area of curved surface of a cone $= \pi r \times$ slant height

Greek letters

Lower case	Upper case	Name	Lower case	Upper case	Name
α	A	alpha	ν	N	nu
β	B	beta	ξ	Ξ	xi
γ	Γ	gamma	o	O	omicron
δ	Δ	delta	π	Π	pi
ϵ	E	epsilon	ρ	P	rho
ζ	Z	zeta	σ	Σ	sigma
η	H	eta	τ	T	tau
θ	Θ	theta	υ	Υ	upsilon
ι	I	iota	φ, ϕ	Φ	phi
κ	K	kappa	χ	X	chi
λ	Λ	lambda	ψ	Ψ	psi
μ	M	mu	ω	Ω	omega

Numbers and sets

Sets of numbers

$\mathbb{N}$ — The set of natural numbers, $\{1, 2, 3, ...\}$
(The set of natural numbers is sometimes taken to include zero.)

$\mathbb{Z}$ — The set of integers, $\{0, \pm 1, \pm 2, \pm 3, ...\}$

$\mathbb{Z}^+$ — The set of positive integers, $\{1, 2, 3, ...\}$

$\mathbb{Z}_n$ — The set of integers modulo n, $\{0, 1, 2, ..., n-1\}$

$\mathbb{Q}$ — The set of rational numbers, $\left\{\frac{p}{q} : p \in \mathbb{Z}, q \in \mathbb{Z}^+\right\}$

$\mathbb{Q}^+$ — The set of positive rational numbers, $\{x \in \mathbb{Q}: x > 0\}$

$\mathbb{Q}_0^+$ — The set of positive rational numbers and zero, $\{x \in \mathbb{Q}: x \geq 0\}$

$\mathbb{R}$ — The set of real numbers

$\mathbb{R}^+$ — The set of positive real numbers, $\{x \in \mathbb{R}: x > 0\}$.

$\mathbb{R}_0^+$ — The set of positive real numbers and zero, $\{x \in \mathbb{R}: x \geq 0\}$

$\mathbb{C}$ — The set of complex numbers (see page 21 for more details)

Modular arithmetic

If counting modulo 7, you would count 1, 2, 3, 4, 5, 6, 0, 1, 2, 3, 4, 5, 6, 0, 1, 2, 3, 4, 5, 6, 0, 1, … . When counting modulo n, all numbers with a factor n are zero.

18 is congruent to 32 (modulo 7) because each of 18 and 32 have the same remainder when divided by 7. Alternatively, their difference, $32 - 18 = 14$, is a multiple of 7. This is written $18 \equiv 32 \pmod 7$.

The modulus of a real number

The modulus of the real number x, denoted $|x|$, is defined as follows.

For $x > 0$, $|x| = x$
For $x < 0$, $|x| = -x$
$|x| < a \iff -a < x < a \ (a > 0)$

Set notation and Venn diagrams

$\in$ — is an element of
$\notin$ — is not an element of
$n(A)$ — the number of elements in set A
A' — the complement of the set A ('not A')
$\cup$ — union
$\cap$ — intersection
$A \subset B$ — A is a proper subset of B (i.e. A is not the same as B)
$A \supset B$ — A is a proper superset of B (i.e. A is not the same as B)
$A \subseteq B$ — A is a subset of B
$A \supseteq B$ — A is a superset of B
$\varnothing$ — the empty set
$\mathscr{C}$ — the universal set

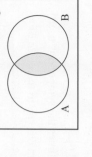

$A \cap B$

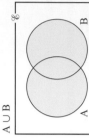

$A \cup B$

A'

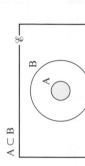

$A \supset B$

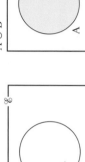

$A \subset B$

Irrational numbers

An irrational number cannot be written in the form $\frac{p}{q}$ where p is an integer and q is a positive integer. Examples of irrational numbers are $\sqrt{2}$ and π.

Algebraic numbers

An algebraic number is a number which can be the root of a polynomial equation with integer coefficients. All rational numbers are algebraic, so are some irrational and complex numbers, for example $\sqrt{2}$ and i.

Transcendental numbers

A transcendental number is a real or complex number that is not the root of any polynomial equation with integer coefficients. π and e are real transcendental numbers.

Surds

A surd is an irrational square root or an expression consisting of the sum or difference of one (or more) irrational square roots and (possibly) rational numbers. Examples include
$\sqrt{7}$; $\sqrt{3} + \sqrt{5}$; $\sqrt{3} + \frac{2}{3}\sqrt{5} - 2$; $3\sqrt{5} + \frac{2}{3}$.

Factorials

For a positive integer n, $n! = n(n-1)(n-2) \times ... \times 2 \times 1$.
$0!$ is defined to be 1.

Symbols and proof

Symbols

$=$	is equal to
$\neq$	is not equal to
$\equiv$	is identically equal to or is congruent to
$\approx$ (or $\simeq$)	is approximately equal to
$\cong$	is isomorphic to
$\propto$	is proportional to, varies as
$<$	is less than
$\leqslant$, $\leq$	is less than or equal to
$\ll$	is much less than
$>$	is greater than
$\geqslant$, $\geq$	is greater than or equal to
$\gg$	is much greater than
$[a, b]$	the set of numbers, x, such that $a \leqslant x \leqslant b$
(a, b)	the set of numbers, x, such that $a < x < b$
(a, ∞)	the set of numbers, x, such that $a < x$
$(a, b]$	the set of numbers, x, such that $a < x \leqslant b$
$\lvert\ \rvert$	modulus
∞	infinity
$\exists$	there exists
$\forall$	for all
$\therefore$	therefore
$\because$	because

Proof

An **identity** is true for all possible values of the variable(s) it contains. For example: $\sin^2\theta + \cos^2\theta = 1$; $(x-y)(x+y) = x^2 - y^2$. The symbol $\equiv$ is sometimes used instead of $=$ in an identity.

$p \Rightarrow q$: 'p implies q' means the same as 'if p is true then q is true' or 'p is a **sufficient** condition for q'; q must happen if p does. For example, 'I am driving somewhere' implies 'I am in a vehicle'.

$p \Leftarrow q$: 'p implied by q' means the same as 'if q is true then p is true' or 'p is a **necessary** condition for q'; p must happen if q does. For example, 'the shape has straight sides' is implied by 'the shape is a hexagon'.

$p \Leftrightarrow q$: 'p implies and is implied by q' means that p is equivalent to q.

Conjecture A statement which may or may not be true; it is usually something you would like to prove. For example, Goldbach's conjecture is the statement: 'Any even number greater than 2 can be written as the sum of two prime numbers'.

A–E

Axiom A general statement accepted without proof. A set of axioms is used to deduce all other results in an area of mathematics.

Proposition A fundamental (proven) statement, underlying the whole area, which is used frequently (e.g. uniqueness of inverses in a group).

Caution: The term 'proposition' has a somewhat different meaning in logic; see page 42.

Lemma An intermediate result which contributes directly to the proof of a particular theorem and which may be useful elsewhere.

Theorem A major result.

Corollary A reasonably immediate consequence of a theorem.

Proof by deduction consists of starting with things you know to be true then proceeding logically, step by step, until you prove your conjecture.

Proof by exhaustion means showing that *all* the possible cases described in the conjecture are true, often separately. The four colour theorem was proved by exhaustion; all possible maps were reduced to a certain number of cases which were then checked individually by a computer. (The four colour theorem states that when colouring maps so that no two adjacent sections are the same colour, no more than four colours will be needed.)

In **proof by contradiction**, the starting point is to assume that the conjecture is false. If it can then be shown that this leads, via a series of correct logical deductions, to a contradictory or untrue statement, the original conjecture must have been true. The most common proof that $\sqrt{2}$ cannot be rational is a proof by contradiction.

The method of **proof by induction** is sometimes used for proving results that are true for all positive integers, n; it consists of four stages.

1 Checking that the result is true for an initial value, usually $n = 1$.

2 Assuming that it is true for $n = k$.

3 Proving that if it is true when $n = k$ then it is also true when $n = k + 1$.

4 Concluding that it is true for all positive integer values of n greater than or equal to the initial value.

A **counter-example** is an example which disproves a conjecture. Its very existence proves that the conjecture is not always true and, hence, disproves it. For example, the number 9 provides a counter-example to the conjecture 'all odd numbers are prime' and so disproves that conjecture.

Algebra

Quadratic equations [A]

$ax^2 + bx + c = 0 \; (a \neq 0) \Rightarrow x = \dfrac{-b \pm \sqrt{b^2 - 4ac}}{2a}$

The **discriminant** is $(b^2 - 4ac)$.   Discriminant > 0: 2 distinct real roots
Discriminant = 0: 1 repeated root
Discriminant < 0: No real roots

The factor theorem [A]

$f(a) = 0 \Leftrightarrow (x - a)$ is a factor of the polynomial $f(x)$.
For example, $x^2 - 3x + 2 = 0$ when $x = 2 \Leftrightarrow (x - 2)$ is a factor of $x^2 - 3x + 2$.

See page 11 for more on polynomials.

The remainder theorem [A]

The remainder when a polynomial $f(x)$ is divided by $(x - a)$ is $f(a)$.

Roots of equations [D]

Quadratics
If $ax^2 + bx + c = 0 \; (a \neq 0)$ has roots α and β, then

$\alpha + \beta = -\dfrac{b}{a}$ and $\alpha\beta = \dfrac{c}{a}$

Cubics
If $ax^3 + bx^2 + cx + d = 0 \; (a \neq 0)$ has roots α, β and γ, then

$\alpha + \beta + \gamma = -\dfrac{b}{a}$ and $\alpha\beta + \beta\gamma + \gamma\alpha = \dfrac{c}{a}$ and $\alpha\beta\gamma = -\dfrac{d}{a}$

Quartics
If $ax^4 + bx^3 + cx^2 + dx + e = 0 \; (a \neq 0)$ has roots α, β, γ and δ, then

$\alpha + \beta + \gamma + \delta = -\dfrac{b}{a}$ and $\alpha\beta + \alpha\gamma + \alpha\delta + \beta\gamma + \beta\delta + \gamma\delta = \dfrac{c}{a}$ and

$\alpha\beta\gamma + \beta\gamma\delta + \gamma\delta\alpha + \delta\alpha\beta = -\dfrac{d}{a}$ and $\alpha\beta\gamma\delta = \dfrac{e}{a}$

There are similar results for higher-order equations.

Equations with some complex roots [D]

If a polynomial equation has real coefficients then any complex roots occur in conjugate pairs; i.e. if $a + bi$ is a root then so is $a - bi$.

The binomial expansion when n is a positive integer [A]

$(a + b)^n = a^n + {}^nC_1 a^{n-1}b + {}^nC_2 a^{n-2}b^2 + \ldots + {}^nC_r a^{n-r}b^r + \ldots + b^n, \qquad n \in \mathbb{N}$

The binomial coefficient

${}^nC_r = \binom{n}{r} = \dfrac{n!}{r!(n-r)!} = \dfrac{n \times (n-1) \times \ldots \times (n-r+1)}{r!}$

${}^nC_0 = {}^nC_n = 1$

Binomial coefficients may also
be found using Pascal's triangle.

$$
\begin{array}{ccccccccc}
 & & & & 1 & & & & \\
 & & & 1 & & 1 & & & \\
 & & 1 & & 2 & & 1 & & \\
 & 1 & & 3 & & 3 & & 1 & \\
1 & & 4 & & 6 & & 4 & & 1 \\
\end{array}
$$

$$
\begin{array}{ccccccccccc}
1 & & 5 & & 10 & & 10 & & 5 & & 1
\end{array}
$$

and so on

Addition of binomial coefficients [B]

${}^nC_r + {}^nC_{r+1} = {}^{n+1}C_{r+1}$

General binomial expansion [B]

$(1 + x)^n = 1 + nx + \dfrac{n(n-1)}{2!}x^2 + \dfrac{n(n-1)(n-2)}{3!}x^3 + \ldots, \qquad |x| < 1, \qquad n \in \mathbb{R}$

$(a + x)^n = a^n \left[1 + \dfrac{x}{a} \right]^n$

$\qquad = a^n \left[1 + n\left(\dfrac{x}{a}\right) + \dfrac{n(n-1)}{2!}\left(\dfrac{x}{a}\right)^2 + \dfrac{n(n-1)(n-2)}{3!}\left(\dfrac{x}{a}\right)^3 + \ldots \right], \qquad \left|\dfrac{x}{a}\right| < 1, \qquad n \in \mathbb{R}$

Partial fractions [B]

$\dfrac{px + q}{(ax + b)(cx + d)} \equiv \dfrac{A}{(ax + b)} + \dfrac{B}{(cx + d)}$

$\dfrac{px^2 + qx + r}{(ax + b)(cx^2 + d)} \equiv \dfrac{A}{(ax + b)} + \dfrac{Bx + C}{(cx^2 + d)}$

$\dfrac{px^2 + qx + r}{(ax + b)(cx + d)^2} \equiv \dfrac{A}{(ax + b)} + \dfrac{B}{(cx + d)} + \dfrac{C}{(cx + d)^2}$

Similar results apply for fractions with any number of factors in the denominator, as long as its degree exceeds that of the numerator.

Indices and logarithms

Indices

A

For $m, n \in \mathbb{R}$

$a^m \times a^n = a^{m+n}$

$a^m \div a^n = a^{m-n}$

$a^0 = 1 \quad (a \neq 0)$

$a^{-m} = \dfrac{1}{a^m} \quad (a \neq 0)$

$a^{\frac{1}{n}} = \sqrt[n]{a} \quad (n \neq 0)$

$(a^m)^n = a^{mn}$

$a^{\frac{m}{n}} = \sqrt[n]{a^m} = \left(\sqrt[n]{a}\right)^m \quad (n \neq 0)$

Logarithms and exponentials

A

$p = a^q \iff q = \log_a p \quad (a > 0)$

$\log_a a = 1$

$\log_a (1) = 0$

$\log_a (xy) = \log_a x + \log_a y$

$\log_a \left(\dfrac{x}{y}\right) = \log_a x - \log_a y$

$\log_a (x^n) = n \log_a x$

$\log_a \left(\sqrt[n]{x}\right) = \dfrac{1}{n} \log_a x$

$\log_a x = \dfrac{\log_b x}{\log_b a}$ (change of base formula)

$\log_a \left(\dfrac{1}{x}\right) = -\log_a x$

Most calculators give both natural logarithms and logarithms to base 10.

The exponential function and natural logarithms

B,C

$y = e^x \iff x = \log_e y = \ln y$

$e^{\ln x} \equiv x \qquad \ln(e^x) \equiv x$

$e^{x \ln a} = a^x$

$e^x = \exp(x) = 1 + x + \dfrac{x^2}{2!} + \ldots + \dfrac{x^r}{r!} + \ldots, \quad \text{all } x$

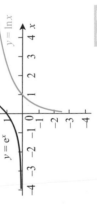

Limits

B,E

As $x \to \infty$: $\ln x \to \infty$, $e^x \to \infty$, $e^{-x} \to 0$

$\displaystyle\lim_{x \to \infty}(x^k e^{-x}) = 0$ for any k; $\quad \displaystyle\lim_{x \to 0}(x^k \ln x) = 0$ for $k > 0$

Using logarithms to reduce graphs to linear form

A

$y = ax^n$

$\log y = n \log x + \log a$

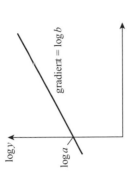

gradient $= n$

$y = ab^x$

$\log y = (\log b)x + \log a$

gradient $= \log b$

Hyperbolic functions

E

$\sinh x = \dfrac{e^x - e^{-x}}{2}$

$\cosh x = \dfrac{e^x + e^{-x}}{2}$

$\tanh x = \dfrac{\sinh x}{\cosh x}$

$\cosh^2 x - \sinh^2 x = 1$

$\text{sech } x = \dfrac{1}{\cosh x} = \dfrac{2}{e^x + e^{-x}}$

$\text{arsinh } x = \sinh^{-1} x = \ln\left(x + \sqrt{x^2 + 1}\right)$

$\text{arcosh } x = \cosh^{-1} x = \ln\left(x + \sqrt{x^2 - 1}\right), \quad x \geqslant 1$

$\text{artanh } x = \tanh^{-1} x = \dfrac{1}{2} \ln\left(\dfrac{1+x}{1-x}\right), \quad |x| < 1$

$\sinh 2x = 2 \sinh x \cosh x$

$\cosh 2x = \cosh^2 x + \sinh^2 x$

$\text{cosech } x = \dfrac{1}{\sinh x} = \dfrac{2}{e^x - e^{-x}}$

$\coth x = \dfrac{\cosh x}{\sinh x}$

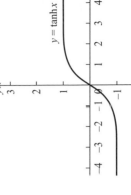

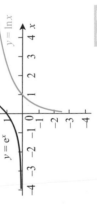

For $x \in \mathbb{R}$: $\cosh x \geqslant 1$, $\sinh x \in \mathbb{R}$, $-1 < \tanh x < 1$

Co-ordinate geometry

Co-ordinates

Abscissa   The x co-ordinate in two-dimensional cartesian co-ordinates.

Ordinate   The y co-ordinate in two-dimensional cartesian co-ordinates.

Straight lines

A, C

The line joining (x_1, y_1) to (x_2, y_2)

Gradient $m = \dfrac{y_2 - y_1}{x_2 - x_1}$ Length $\sqrt{(x_2 - x_1)^2 + (y_2 - y_1)^2}$

Equation $\dfrac{y - y_1}{x - x_1} = \dfrac{y_2 - y_1}{x_2 - x_1}$ Mid-point $\left(\dfrac{x_1 + x_2}{2}, \dfrac{y_1 + y_2}{2} \right)$

Other forms of the equation of a straight line

Through (x_1, y_1) with gradient m: $y - y_1 = m(x - x_1)$

Through $(0, c)$ with gradient m: $y = mx + c$

Through $(a, 0)$ and $(0, b)$: $\dfrac{x}{a} + \dfrac{y}{b} = 1$

Perpendicular lines: The product of their gradients is -1 (unless they are parallel to the axes).

Parallel lines: Their gradients are equal.

The perpendicular distance of the point (x_1, y_1) from the line $ax + by + c = 0$

$$\dfrac{|ax_1 + by_1 + c|}{\sqrt{a^2 + b^2}}$$

Circles and right angles

A

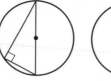

The angle in a semi-circle is a right angle.

The line from the centre of a circle perpendicular to a chord bisects that chord.

A tangent to a circle is perpendicular to the radius at the point of contact.

The circle

B

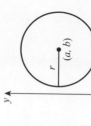

The cartesian equation of a circle with centre (a, b) and radius r is

$$(x - a)^2 + (y - b)^2 = r^2.$$

Parametric equations: $x = a + r\cos\theta$ $y = b + r\sin\theta$

The circle with the equation $x^2 + y^2 + 2gx + 2fy + c = 0$ has its centre at $(-g, -f)$ and a radius of length $\sqrt{g^2 + f^2 - c}$.

Curves

Features of curves B, E

An **asymptote** can be thought of as a 'tangent at infinity'; it is a line that the curve gets nearer to as either x or y approaches infinity.

An asymptote which is not parallel to one of the co-ordinate axes is called an **oblique asymptote**.

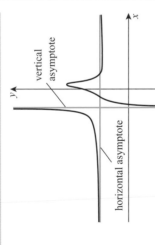

vertical asymptote

horizontal asymptote

A **cusp** is a point where two parts of a curve meet. There may be a common tangent at the cusp, e.g. $x^5 - y^2 = 0$, or the curve may be non-differentiable at the cusp, e.g. $y = (|x| - 2)^2$.

cusp

$x^5 - y^2 = 0$

cusp

$y = (|x| - 2)^2$

A **node** is a point where a curve crosses itself, often forming a **loop**.

node

loop

$x^5 - y^2 + x^2 = 0$

A **dimple** can be described as an indentation on a curve, as shown.

node

$r = 2\cos\theta + 1$

cusp

$r = \cos\theta + 1$

dimple

$r = 0.7\cos\theta + 1$

Polar co-ordinates E

The position of a point P is defined by its distance, r, from a fixed point, O (the pole), and the angle, θ, that OP makes with the initial line.

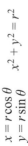

(x, y)

$x = r\cos\theta$
$y = r\sin\theta$ $x^2 + y^2 = r^2$

The **principal polar co-ordinates** of a point have $r > 0$ and $-\pi < \theta \leqslant \pi$.

Conics E

A **conic** is a curve which may be produced by slicing a cone with a plane surface. For any point on the conic, the distance from the **focus** (a fixed point) is the **eccentricity** multiplied by the distance from the **directrix** (a fixed line).

The first row in the table below gives the standard forms of the equations of some conics. You will also come across transformations of the conics; for example, the curve with equation $x^2 - y^2 = 1$ is a hyperbola with perpendicular axes and is, therefore, a rectangular hyperbola, even though its cartesian equation is not in the form $xy = c^2$.

Type of conic	Ellipse $a > b$	Parabola	Hyperbola	Rectangular hyperbola
Standard form	$\dfrac{x^2}{a^2} + \dfrac{y^2}{b^2} = 1$	$y^2 = 4ax$	$\dfrac{x^2}{a^2} - \dfrac{y^2}{b^2} = 1$	$xy = c^2$
Parametric form	$(a\cos\theta, b\sin\theta)$	$(at^2, 2at)$	$(a\sec\theta, b\tan\theta)$	$\left(ct, \dfrac{c}{t}\right)$
Eccentricity	$0 < e < 1$ $b^2 = a^2(1 - e^2)$	$e = 1$	$e > 1$ $b^2 = a^2(e^2 - 1)$	$e = \sqrt{2}$
Foci	$(\pm ae, 0)$	$(a, 0)$	$(\pm ae, 0)$	$(\pm c\sqrt{2}, \pm c\sqrt{2})$
Directrices	$x = \pm\dfrac{a}{e}$	$x = -a$	$x = \pm\dfrac{a}{e}$	$x + y = \pm c\sqrt{2}$
Asymptotes	none	none	$\dfrac{x}{a} = \pm\dfrac{y}{b}$	$x = 0, y = 0$

Any of these conics can be expressed in polar co-ordinates (with the focus as the origin) as $\dfrac{l}{r} = 1 + e\cos\theta$ where l is the length of the **semi-latus rectum**.

The **semi-latus rectum** is a line from the focus to the conic, parallel to the directrix.

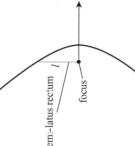

semi-latus rectum l

focus

The complete family of conics also includes the circle ($e = 0$), point and pair of intersecting straight lines.

The curves in the table, and many others, are illustrated in the Glossary of curves on pages 8–10.

Glossary of curves

Circle $x = a\cos t, y = a\sin t$ or $x^2 + y^2 = a^2$

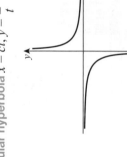

Parabola $x = at^2, y = 2at$ or $y^2 = 4ax$

Ellipse $x = a\cos t, y = b\sin t$ or $\dfrac{x^2}{a^2} + \dfrac{y^2}{b^2} = 1$

Hyperbola $x = a\sec t, y = b\tan t$ or $\dfrac{x^2}{a^2} - \dfrac{y^2}{b^2} = 1$

Rectangular hyperbola $x = ct, y = \dfrac{c}{t}$ or $xy = c^2$

Cycloid $x = a(t - \sin t), y = a(1 - \cos t)$

Curtate cycloid
$x = at - b\sin t, y = a - b\cos t$ where $b < a$

Prolate cycloid
$x = at - b\sin t, y = a - b\cos t$ where $b > a$

Epicycloid $x = ka\cos t - a\cos kt, y = ka\sin t - a\sin kt$

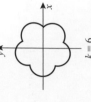

$k = 6$

Hypocycloid $x = ka\cos t + a\cos kt, y = ka\sin t - a\sin kt$

$k = 5$

Cardioid $r = 2a(1 + \cos\theta)$

Nephroid $x = 3a\cos t - a\cos 3t, y = 3a\sin t - a\sin 3t$

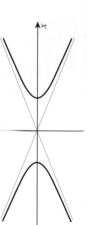

Glossary of curves

Lemniscate $r^2 = a^2 \cos 2\theta$

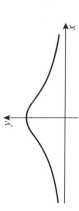

Folium of Descartes $x^3 + y^3 = 3axy$

Eight curve $r^2 = \cos 2\theta \sec^4 \theta$

Witch of Agnesi $x = 2a \tan t, y = 2a \cos^2 t$

Limaçon $r = 2a \cos \theta + k$

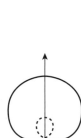

$k = a$

Trisectrix of Maclaurin $r = 2a \dfrac{\sin 3\theta}{\sin 2\theta}$

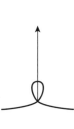

Lissajous curves $x = a \sin(ct + d), y = b \sin t$

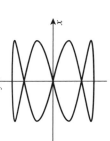

$a = 1, b = 1, c = 4, d = 0$

Archimedes' spiral $r = k\theta$

Conchoid of Nicomedes $r = a \sec \theta + k$

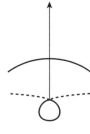

Astroid $x^{\frac{2}{3}} + y^{\frac{2}{3}} = a^{\frac{2}{3}}$

Right strophoid $x = \dfrac{a(t^2 - 1)}{t^2 + 1}, y = \dfrac{at(t^2 - 1)}{t^2 + 1}$

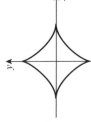

Cissoid of Diocles $r = 2a(\sec \theta - \cos \theta)$

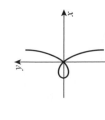

Glossary of curves

Deltoid $x = 2a\cos t + a\cos 2t$, $y = 2a\sin t + a\sin 2t$

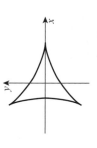

The **envelope** of a family of curves is the curve that touches every curve in the family. In the diagram below, a cardioid touches each member of a family of circles. See also page 16.

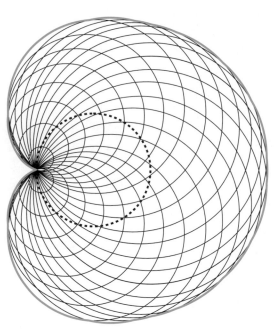

Important features of curves to recognise

● Symmetry and periodicity

● Vertical, horizontal and oblique asymptotes

● Cusps, loops and dimples

● Nodes (or crossover points)

To sketch a cartesian curve, draw a diagram, not necessarily to scale and not usually on graph paper, showing its main features.

● Turning points

● Asymptotes

● Intersection with the y axis

● Intersection with the x axis

● Behaviour for large x (+ and −)

For curves given in **cartesian** or **parametric** form, calculus techniques are used to find

● the equations of tangents and normals

● the maximum and minimum values of x and y

● the maximum and minimum distances of a curve from the origin.

Curves given in **polar** form are sometimes drawn with parts of the curve where $r > 0$ as a solid line and $r < 0$ as a broken line. Calculus techniques are used to find

● the maximum and minimum distances of the curve from the pole

● the points on the curve where the tangent is parallel, or perpendicular, to the initial line.

Trident $xy = x^3 - a^3$

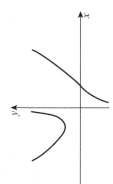

Kappa curve $r = a\cot\theta$

Maltese cross $xy(x^2 - y^2) = x^2 + y^2$

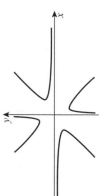

Piriform $x = a(1 + \sin t)$, $y = \dfrac{a}{k}\cos t(1 + \sin t)$

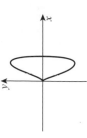

Functions

Mappings and functions [B]

A mapping associates the elements of one set (the **domain**) with those of another set (the **co-domain**). The outcome from applying a mapping to a particular element is its **image**. In general an element may have more than one image. In the example in the diagram, the domain is a set of quadrilaterals and the co-domain is the set of vowels.

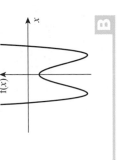

A **function** is a mapping in which each element of the domain has a unique image in the co-domain.
A function may be a **one-to-one** or a **many-to-one** mapping.

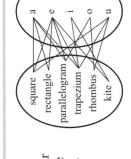

one-to-one   many-to-one

If input is plotted on the x axis and output on the y axis then, for functions that are graphed as curves, any line parallel to the y axis crosses the curve at most once.

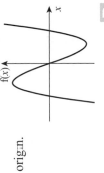

For a **one-to-one function** there is only one input for each output: any line parallel to the y axis or the x axis crosses the curve at most once.

For a **many-to-one function**, although there is only one possible output for each input, there is more than one input for at least one output.

The **range** is the set of all possible images and is a subset of the co-domain. For example, the function 'square' maps the domain of real numbers on to the co-domain of real numbers but the range is non-negative real numbers.

Composition of functions A combination of two (or more) functions, in which one function is applied to the result of another. For the composite function fg(x), first apply g to x, then apply f to the result.

Inverse functions [B]

The inverse of a function f is the function which reverses the effect of f. A function only has an inverse if it is one-to-one and the co-domain equals the range. The graph of the inverse function, $y = f^{-1}(x)$, is the reflection of the graph of $y = f(x)$ in the line $y = x$.

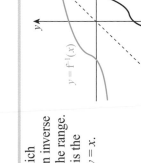
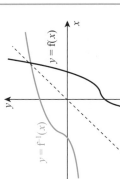

Monotonic functions [B]

A (strictly) monotonic function is either increasing or decreasing. For an increasing function, as x increases, so does f(x): the gradient of the graph of f(x) against x is always positive. For a decreasing function, as x increases, f(x) decreases: the gradient of the graph of f(x) against x is always negative.

Even functions [B]

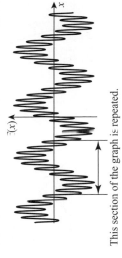

For an even function, f(−x) = f(x) for all x.
The graph of y = f(x) is symmetrical about the y axis.

Odd functions [B]

For an odd function, f(−x) = −f(x) for all x.
The graph of y = f(x) has rotation symmetry about the origin.

Periodic functions [B]

The graph of a periodic function 'keeps repeating'.
For any periodic function there is some non-zero value of k for which f(x + k) = f(x) for all values of x. The period of the function is defined to be the smallest such value of k.

This section of the graph is repeated.
This distance is k

Polynomial [A]

A polynomial is an expression which involves positive integer powers and constants only; for example, $3x^3 - 5x + 1$ is a polynomial. $5x^2 + \frac{1}{x}$ is not a polynomial since $\frac{1}{x} = x^{-1}$ and −1 is not a positive integer.

The **degree** (order) of a polynomial is the greatest power of the variable. For example, the degree of $3x^2 - 5x$ is 2; the degree of $3 - 4y + 3y^5$ is 5.

Functions

Functions

Transforming graphs

A

$y = f(ax)$ is a stretch of $y = f(x)$, scale factor $\frac{1}{a}$ parallel to the x axis ($a > 1$ in the diagram)

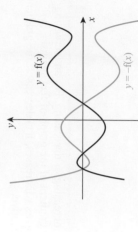

$y = af(x)$ is a stretch of $y = f(x)$, scale factor a parallel to the y axis ($a > 1$ in the diagram)

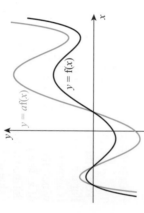

$y = f(x + a)$ is a translation of $y = f(x)$ a units to the left ($a > 0$ in the diagram)

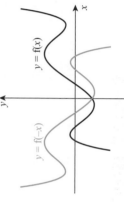

$y = f(x) + a$ is a translation of $y = f(x)$ a units up ($a > 0$ in the diagram)

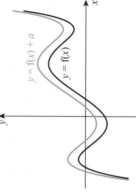

$y = -f(x)$ is a reflection of $y = f(x)$ in the x axis

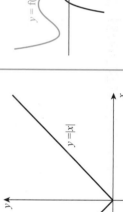

$y = f(-x)$ is a reflection of $y = f(x)$ in the y axis

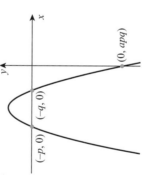

Quadratic graphs

A

In these diagrams, $p > 0$ and $q > 0$.

$y = a(x + p)^2 + q$ for $a > 0$
$x = -p$ is a line of symmetry

$y = a(x + p)^2 + q$ for $a < 0$
$x = -p$ is a line of symmetry

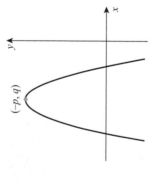

$y = a(x + p)(x + q)$ for $a > 0$

$y = a(x + p)(x + q)$ for $a < 0$

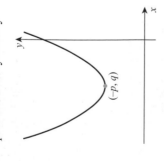

The modulus function

B

The modulus of the real number x, denoted $|x|$, is defined as follows.

For $x > 0$, $|x| = x$
For $x < 0$, $|x| = -x$

12

Sequences and series

Sequences and series

A sequence is an ordered list; for example, 3, 6, 10, 15, ... It can be finite or infinite. The kth term of a sequence is often denoted with a suffix (u_k, T_k, a_k).
A series is the sum of consecutive terms in a sequence, starting from a first term.

Arithmetic sequences and series

In an **arithmetic sequence** (or **progression**), each term is the previous term plus a fixed number called the **common difference**. For example, 4, 6, 8, 10, ... is an arithmetic sequence with common difference 2.

For the arithmetic sequence $a, a + d, a + 2d, ..., a + (n-1)d$

General (kth) term, $u_k = a + (k-1)d$
Last (nth) term, $l = u_n = a + (n-1)d$
Sum of all n terms, $S_n = \frac{n}{2}(a+l) = \frac{n}{2}[2a + (n-1)d]$

Geometric sequences and series

In a **geometric sequence** (or **progression**), each term is the previous term multiplied by a fixed number called the **common ratio**. For example, 4, 8, 16, 32, ... is a geometric sequence with common ratio 2.

For the geometric sequence $a, ar, ar^2, ...$

General (kth) term, $u_k = ar^{k-1}$

Sum to n terms, $S_n = \frac{a(1-r^n)}{1-r} = \frac{a(r^n - 1)}{r-1}$

Sum to infinity, $S_\infty = \frac{a}{1-r}$ $-1 < r < 1$

A convergent sequence tends to a limit; that is, the terms get closer and closer to a certain value. For example, the terms of the sequence 0.3, 0.33, 0.333, 0.3333, 0.333 33, ... converge to $\frac{1}{3}$. A convergent series has a sum to infinity; that is, there is a limit to the sum to n terms as $n \to \infty$.

In a divergent sequence, the terms do not tend to a limit. For example 1, 2, 3, 4, 5, 6, ... is a divergent sequence. For a divergent series, there is no limit to the sum to n terms as $n \to \infty$.

Note that $1, \frac{1}{2}, \frac{1}{3}, \frac{1}{4}, ...$ is a convergent sequence but $1 + \frac{1}{2} + \frac{1}{3} + \frac{1}{4} + ...$ is a divergent series. $1 - 1 + 1 - 1 + 1 - 1 ...$ is also a divergent series.

In a periodic sequence, a finite number of terms keeps repeating. For example, 1, 3, 2, 4, 8, 1, 3, 2, 4, 8, 1, 3, 2, 4, 8, ... is a periodic sequence with period 5.

Summation

$$\sum_{i=1}^{n} x_i = x_1 + x_2 + ... + x_n$$

Product

$$\prod_{i=1}^{n} x_i = x_1 x_2 ... x_n$$

Finite series

$$\sum_{r=1}^{n} r = \frac{1}{2}n(n+1) \qquad \sum_{r=1}^{n} r^2 = \frac{1}{6}n(n+1)(2n+1) \qquad \sum_{r=1}^{n} r^3 = \frac{1}{4}n^2(n+1)^2$$

Infinite series

Maclaurin: $f(x) = f(0) + xf'(0) + \frac{x^2}{2!}f''(0) + ... + \frac{x^r}{r!}f^{(r)}(0) + ...$

Taylor: $f(x) = f(a) + (x-a)f'(a) + \frac{(x-a)^2}{2!}f''(a) + ... + \frac{(x-a)^r}{r!}f^{(r)}(a) + ...$

$f(a+x) = f(a) + xf'(a) + \frac{x^2}{2!}f''(a) + ... + \frac{x^r}{r!}f^{(r)}(a) + ...$

$e^x = 1 + x + \frac{x^2}{2!} + ... + \frac{x^r}{r!} + ...$,   all x

$\ln(1+x) = x - \frac{x^2}{2} + \frac{x^3}{3} - ... + (-1)^{r+1}\frac{x^r}{r} + ...$, $-1 < x \leqq 1$

$\sin x = x - \frac{x^3}{3!} + \frac{x^5}{5!} - ... + (-1)^r \frac{x^{2r+1}}{(2r+1)!} + ...$,   all x

$\cos x = 1 - \frac{x^2}{2!} + \frac{x^4}{4!} - ... + (-1)^r \frac{x^{2r}}{(2r)!} + ...$,   all x

$\arctan x = x - \frac{x^3}{3} + \frac{x^5}{5} - ... + (-1)^r \frac{x^{2r+1}}{2r+1} + ...$, $-1 \leqq x \leqq 1$

$\sinh x = x + \frac{x^3}{3!} + \frac{x^5}{5!} + ... + \frac{x^{2r+1}}{(2r+1)!} + ...$,   all x

$\cosh x = 1 + \frac{x^2}{2!} + \frac{x^4}{4!} + ... + \frac{x^{2r}}{(2r)!} + ...$,   all x

$\text{artanh } x = x + \frac{x^3}{3} + \frac{x^5}{5} + ... + \frac{x^{2r+1}}{2r+1} + ...$, $-1 < x < 1$

General binomial expansion:
$(1+x)^n = 1 + nx + \frac{n(n-1)}{2!}x^2 + \frac{n(n-1)(n-2)}{3!}x^3 + ...$, $|x| < 1, n \in \mathbb{R}$

Calculus

Differentiation

Notation The derivative of $y = f(x)$ may be denoted by $\dfrac{dy}{dx}$ or $f'(x)$.

Other common notations are y' for $\dfrac{dy}{dx}$ and $\dot{y}$ for $\dfrac{dy}{dt}$.

For $y = x^n$, $\quad \dfrac{dy}{dx} = nx^{n-1}$

For $y = f(x) + g(x)$, $\quad \dfrac{dy}{dx} = f'(x) + g'(x)$

Differentiation of $y = f(x)$ from first principles

$$\frac{dy}{dx} = \lim_{\delta x \to 0} \frac{\delta y}{\delta x} = \lim_{\delta x \to 0} \frac{f(x + \delta x) - f(x)}{\delta x}$$

i.e. The gradient of the tangent at a point P is the limit of the gradient of chord PQ as Q approaches P.

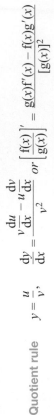

Tangents and normals

A **tangent** to a curve is a straight line with the same gradient as the curve at the point of contact.

A **normal** to a curve is a straight line at right angles to the tangent at the point of contact.

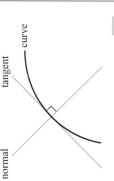

Stationary points

At a stationary point $\dfrac{dy}{dx} = 0$;

$\dfrac{d^2y}{dx^2} < 0 \Rightarrow$ maximum; $\dfrac{d^2y}{dx^2} > 0 \Rightarrow$ minimum;

$\dfrac{d^2y}{dx^2} = 0 \Rightarrow$ minimum *or* maximum *or* stationary point of inflection (needs further investigation)

Sign of gradient near stationary point

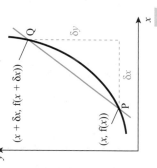

Point of inflection

A point at which a curve starts to curve in the opposite direction. If the gradient of the curve at the point of inflection is zero, it is a stationary point of inflection; otherwise, it is a non-stationary point of inflection.

At a point of inflection, the second derivative is zero (unless it is undefined). However, the second derivative can be zero at a maximum or a minimum point.

Further differentiation

Product rule $\quad y = uv, \quad \dfrac{dy}{dx} = u\dfrac{dv}{dx} + v\dfrac{du}{dx}$ or $[f(x)g(x)]' = f(x)g'(x) + f'(x)g(x)$

Quotient rule $\quad y = \dfrac{u}{v}, \quad \dfrac{dy}{dx} = \dfrac{v\dfrac{du}{dx} - u\dfrac{dv}{dx}}{v^2}$ or $\left[\dfrac{f(x)}{g(x)}\right]' = \dfrac{g(x)f'(x) - f(x)g'(x)}{[g(x)]^2}$

Chain rule $\quad y = f(u), u = g(x), \quad \dfrac{dy}{dx} = \dfrac{dy}{du} \times \dfrac{du}{dx}$ or $\{f[g(x)]\}' = f'[g(x)]g'(x)$

Inverse function $\quad \dfrac{dx}{dy} = 1 \div \dfrac{dy}{dx}$

Integration

$$\int x^n \, dx = \frac{x^{n+1}}{n+1} + c, \quad n \neq -1$$

$$\int \frac{1}{x} \, dx = \ln|x| + c$$

$$\int (f'(x) + g'(x)) \, dx = f(x) + g(x) + c$$

Definite integrals

$\int_a^b f(x) \, dx$ gives the area of the region bounded by $y = f(x)$, the x axis and the lines $x = a$ and $x = b$, with the area being positive above the x axis and negative below it.

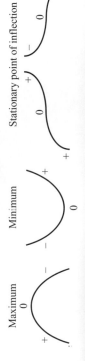

$$\int_a^b f(x) \, dx + \int_b^c f(x) \, dx = \int_a^c f(x) \, dx$$

$$\int_b^a f(x) \, dx = -\int_a^b f(x) \, dx$$

Calculus

The area between a curve and the y axis

$$\int_c^d x \, dy$$

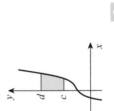

The area between two curves

The area between the curves $y = f(x)$ and $y = g(x)$

is $\int_a^b (f(x) - g(x)) \, dx$

Techiques for integration

Integration by substitution
Some expressions can be integrated if a suitable substitution is made, e.g. $\int_0^{\frac{1}{2}} \frac{1}{\sqrt{1-x^2}} dx$

Substituting $x = \sin\theta$ transforms the integral into $\int_0^{\frac{\pi}{6}} \frac{\cos\theta \, d\theta}{\sqrt{1 - \sin^2\theta}} = \int_0^{\frac{\pi}{6}} d\theta = \frac{\pi}{6}$.

This process is called **integration by substitution**. Notice that the limits must also be changed.

Special case: $\int \frac{g'(x)}{g(x)} dx = \ln|g(x)| + c$ e.g. $\int \frac{4x+1}{2x^2 + x} dx = \ln|2x^2 + x| + c$

Integration by parts $\int u \frac{dv}{dx} dx = uv - \int v \frac{du}{dx} dx$

Volumes of revolution

About the x axis $\int_a^b \pi y^2 \, dx$

About the y axis $\int_p^q \pi x^2 \, dy$

The area of a sector

$A = \frac{1}{2} \int r^2 \, d\theta$ (polar co-ordinates)

$A = \frac{1}{2} \int (x\dot{y} - y\dot{x}) \, dt$ (parametric form, with parameter t)

Integration using parametric equations

The area between a curve and the x axis

$\int_{t_1}^{t_2} y \frac{dx}{dt} \, dt$ (for parameter t)

The volume of a solid of revolution

$\int_{t_1}^{t_2} \pi y^2 \frac{dx}{dt} \, dt$ (this is about the x axis, for parameter t)

Arc length

$s = \int \sqrt{\dot{x}^2 + \dot{y}^2} \, dt$ (parametric form, with parameter t)

$s = \int \sqrt{1 + \left(\frac{dy}{dx}\right)^2} \, dx$ (cartesian co-ordinates)

$s = \int \sqrt{r^2 + \left(\frac{dr}{d\theta}\right)^2} \, d\theta$ (polar co-ordinates)

The surface area of a solid of revolution

About the x axis: $S_x = 2\pi \int y \, ds = 2\pi \int y \sqrt{1 + \left(\frac{dy}{dx}\right)^2} \, dx = 2\pi \int y \sqrt{\dot{x}^2 + \dot{y}^2} \, dt$

About the y axis: $S_y = 2\pi \int x \, ds = 2\pi \int x \sqrt{1 + \left(\frac{dy}{dx}\right)^2} \, dx = 2\pi \int x \sqrt{\dot{x}^2 + \dot{y}^2} \, dt$

$S_y = 2\pi \int x \sqrt{1 + \left(\frac{dx}{dy}\right)^2} \, dy$

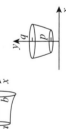

The mean value of a function

The mean value of the function $f(x)$ over the interval $a \leq x \leq b$ is

$\frac{1}{b-a} \int_a^b f(x) \, dx$, $a \neq b$

Calculus

Multivariable calculus

The operator grad

For a function $w = g(x, y, z)$ the vector **grad** g is defined to be:

$$\mathbf{grad}\, g = \begin{vmatrix} \dfrac{\partial g}{\partial x} \\[6pt] \dfrac{\partial g}{\partial y} \\[6pt] \dfrac{\partial g}{\partial z} \end{vmatrix} \quad \text{(may be written } \nabla g\text{).}$$

When evaluated at a point (x, y, z) it gives the magnitude and direction of the greatest rate of change of $w = g(x, y, z)$ at that point.

The tangent plane and the normal line at a point

The **tangent plane** to a three-dimensional surface touches the surface and contains the tangents of all possible sections of the surface through that point. The **normal line** is the line at right angles to the tangent plane. The diagram shows the tangent plane and normal line at point A.

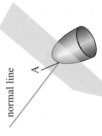

normal line

A

tangent plane

For the point A with a position vector **a** on the surface $g(x, y, z) = k$

the normal line is $\mathbf{r} = \mathbf{a} + \lambda\, \mathbf{grad}\, g$
the tangent plane is $(\mathbf{r} - \mathbf{a}) \cdot \mathbf{grad}\, g = 0$

where **grad** g is evaluated at A.

$$\delta w \approx \frac{\partial w}{\partial x}\delta x + \frac{\partial w}{\partial y}\delta y + \frac{\partial w}{\partial z}\delta z \quad \text{for small } \delta x,\ \delta y,\ \delta z$$

For the surface $z = f(x, y)$ the tangent plane at the point (a, b, c) is
$$z - c = \frac{\partial f}{\partial x}(x - a) + \frac{\partial f}{\partial y}(y - b)$$ with the partial derivatives evaluated at (a, b, c).

A **section** of the three-dimensional surface, given in the form $z = f(x, y)$, is the curve which would be seen if the surface was cut with a plane.

A **saddle point** is a stationary point on a three-dimensional surface, $z = f(x, y)$, such that moving away from it in some directions leads to z increasing but moving away from it in other directions leads to z decreasing.

Envelopes

The **envelope** of a family of curves is the curve that touches every curve in the family. In the diagram on the right, a curve is shown touching a family of straight lines.

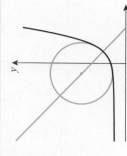

The **envelope** of a family of curves $f(x, y, p) = 0$ is found by

solving simultaneously $f(x, y, p) = 0$ and $\dfrac{\partial}{\partial p} f(x, y, p) = 0$.

Intrinsic co-ordinates

$$\frac{dy}{dx} = \tan\psi \qquad \frac{dx}{ds} = \cos\psi \qquad \frac{dy}{ds} = \sin\psi$$

Tangential unit vector $\hat{\mathbf{t}} = \begin{pmatrix} \cos\psi \\ \sin\psi \end{pmatrix}$

Normal unit vector $\hat{\mathbf{n}} = \begin{pmatrix} -\sin\psi \\ \cos\psi \end{pmatrix}$

Curvature

$$\kappa = \frac{d\psi}{ds} = \frac{\dot{x}\ddot{y} - \ddot{x}\dot{y}}{(\dot{x}^2 + \dot{y}^2)^{\frac{3}{2}}} = \frac{\dfrac{d^2y}{dx^2}}{\left(1 + \left[\dfrac{dy}{dx}\right]^2\right)^{\frac{3}{2}}}$$

Radius of curvature $\rho = \dfrac{1}{\kappa}$

The centre of curvature has position vector $\mathbf{c} = \mathbf{r} + \rho\hat{\mathbf{n}}$

The circle of curvature at a point

The **circle of curvature** is the circle whose centre lies on the normal to the curve and which has the same curvature as the curve at that point.

The **evolute** of a curve is the locus of the centre of curvature; it is also the envelope of the normals.

Calculus

Differentiation

$f(x)$	$f'(x)$
kx^n	knx^{n-1}
e^{kx}	ke^{kx}
a^x	$a^x \ln a$
$\ln x$	$\dfrac{1}{x}$
$\ln[g(x)]$	$\dfrac{g'(x)}{g(x)}$
$\sin kx$	$k\cos kx$
$\cos kx$	$-k\sin kx$
$\tan kx$	$k\sec^2 kx$
$\sec x$	$\sec x \tan x$
$\cot x$	$-\cosec^2 x$
$\cosec x$	$-\cosec x \cot x$
$\arcsin x$	$\dfrac{1}{\sqrt{1-x^2}}$
$\arccos x$	$-\dfrac{1}{\sqrt{1-x^2}}$
$\arctan x$	$\dfrac{1}{1+x^2}$
$\sinh x$	$\cosh x$
$\cosh x$	$\sinh x$
$\tanh x$	$\sech^2 x$
$\arsinh x$	$\dfrac{1}{\sqrt{1+x^2}}$
$\arcosh x$	$\dfrac{1}{\sqrt{x^2-1}}$
$\artanh x$	$\dfrac{1}{1-x^2}$

Integration

$f(x)$	$\int f(x)\,dx$ (+ a constant)
kx^n	$\dfrac{kx^{n+1}}{n+1}, \quad n \neq -1$
e^{kx}	$\dfrac{1}{k}e^{kx}$
$\dfrac{1}{x}$	$\ln|x|, \quad x \neq 0$
$\dfrac{g'(x)}{g(x)}$	$\ln|g(x)|$
$\sin kx$	$-\dfrac{1}{k}\cos kx$
$\cos kx$	$\dfrac{1}{k}\sin kx$
$\sec^2 kx$	$\dfrac{1}{k}\tan kx$
$\tan x$	$\ln|\sec x|$
$\cot x$	$\ln|\sin x|$
$\cosec x$	$-\ln|\cosec x + \cot x| = \ln\left|\tan\dfrac{x}{2}\right|$
$\sec x$	$\ln|\sec x + \tan x| = \ln\left|\tan\left(\dfrac{x}{2}+\dfrac{\pi}{4}\right)\right|$
$\dfrac{1}{x^2-a^2}$	$\dfrac{1}{2a}\ln\left|\dfrac{x-a}{x+a}\right|$
$\dfrac{1}{\sqrt{a^2-x^2}}$	$\arcsin\left(\dfrac{x}{a}\right), \quad |x|<a$
$\dfrac{1}{a^2+x^2}$	$\dfrac{1}{a}\arctan\left(\dfrac{x}{a}\right)$
$\dfrac{1}{a^2-x^2}$	$\dfrac{1}{2a}\ln\left|\dfrac{a+x}{a-x}\right| = \dfrac{1}{a}\artanh\left(\dfrac{x}{a}\right), \quad |x|<a, a>0$
$\sinh x$	$\cosh x$
$\cosh x$	$\sinh x$
$\tanh x$	$\ln\cosh x$
$\dfrac{1}{\sqrt{a^2+x^2}}$	$\arsinh\left(\dfrac{x}{a}\right)$ or $\ln\left(x+\sqrt{x^2+a^2}\right)$
$\dfrac{1}{\sqrt{x^2-a^2}}$	$\arcosh\left(\dfrac{x}{a}\right)$ or $\ln\left(x+\sqrt{x^2-a^2}\right) \quad x>a>0$
$\sin^2 x$	$\dfrac{1}{2}\left(x-\dfrac{1}{2}\sin 2x\right)$

Differential equations

Kinematics

[E]

$$v = \frac{ds}{dt} \qquad a = \frac{dv}{dt} = \frac{d^2s}{dt^2} \qquad a = v\frac{dv}{ds}$$

The integrating factor method

[E]

For $\frac{dy}{dx} + Py = Q$, where P, Q are functions of x only

the integrating factor is $R = e^{\int P dx}$

The solution, y, satisfies the equation $Ry = \int RQ\, dx$.

Tangent fields

[E]

The tangent field for a differential equation shows the gradient of the tangent to the solution curve at each point in space. Each of the dashes used to show a gradient is called a direction indicator.

Isoclines

[E]

An isocline for a differential equation is a line or curve along which the gradient, given by the differential equation, is constant. For example, for the differential equation $\frac{dy}{dx} = 3x$, isoclines would be of the form $3x = c$, where c is a constant.

Numerical solution

See page 28.

Oscillations (including SHM)

See page 34.

Linear differential equations

[E]

For $\frac{d^2y}{dx^2} + a\frac{dy}{dx} + by = f(x)$ where a, b are constants

Homogeneous equation: $f(x) = 0$
Non-homogeneous equation: $f(x) \neq 0$

The auxiliary equation is $\lambda^2 + a\lambda + b = 0$ with roots λ_1 and λ_2.
For the general solution, a **complementary function** and a **particular integral** are required.

The complementary function (C.F.) satisfies the equation with f(x) replaced by zero.

$$y = Ae^{\lambda_1 x} + Be^{\lambda_2 x} \qquad \text{if } \lambda_1 \text{ and } \lambda_2 \text{ are real, } \lambda_1 \neq \lambda_2$$
$$y = Ae^{\lambda x} + Bxe^{\lambda x} \qquad \text{if } \lambda_1 \text{ and } \lambda_2 \text{ are real, } \lambda_1 = \lambda_2 = \lambda$$
$$y = e^{\alpha x}(A\sin\beta x + B\cos\beta x) \qquad \text{if } \lambda_1 = \alpha + \beta i, \lambda_2 = \alpha - \beta i$$

A particular integral (P.I.) is any function which satisfies the full equation.

The general solution is $y = $ C.F. + P.I.

Finding a particular integral

f(x)	Trial function for P.I.
linear function	$lx + m$
polynomial of order n	$a_n x^n + a_{n-1}x^{n-1} + a_{n-2}x^{n-2} + \ldots + a_1 x + a_0$
$c\sin px + d\cos px$ (one of c or d could equal zero)	$l\sin px + m\cos px$
multiple of e^{kx}	ce^{kx}

If the suggested trial function is already part of the complementary function, it will not produce a particular integral; trying the suggestion above multiplied by x (or x^2) will usually produce a suitable P.I.

Trigonometry

Triangles

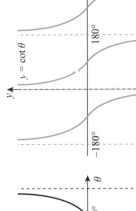

$$\text{Area} = \tfrac{1}{2}ab\sin C = \tfrac{1}{2}bc\sin A = \tfrac{1}{2}ca\sin B$$

$$\text{or area} = \sqrt{s(s-a)(s-b)(s-c)} \quad \text{where } s = \frac{a+b+c}{2}$$

$$\text{Sine rule:} \quad \frac{a}{\sin A} = \frac{b}{\sin B} = \frac{c}{\sin C} = 2R$$

where R is the radius of the circumcircle

$$\text{Cosine rule:} \quad \cos A = \frac{b^2 + c^2 - a^2}{2bc}$$

$$a^2 = b^2 + c^2 - 2bc\cos A$$

Trigonometrical graphs

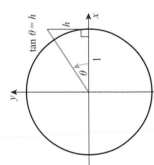

$y = \sin\theta$

$y = \cos\theta$

$y = \cosec\theta$

$y = \sec\theta$

$y = \tan\theta$

$y = \cot\theta$

Trigonometrical identities

$$\frac{\sin\theta}{\cos\theta} = \tan\theta \qquad \sec\theta = \frac{1}{\cos\theta} \qquad \cosec\theta = \frac{1}{\sin\theta} \qquad \cot\theta = \frac{1}{\tan\theta}$$

$$\sin^2\theta + \cos^2\theta = 1 \qquad \tan^2\theta + 1 = \sec^2\theta \qquad 1 + \cot^2\theta = \cosec^2\theta$$

Trigonometrical ratios for acute angles

$$\sin\theta = \frac{b}{c}$$
$$\cos\theta = \frac{a}{c}$$
$$\tan\theta = \frac{b}{a}$$

Trigonometrical ratios for any angle

Consider a circle of radius 1

$$\sin\theta = b$$
$$\cos\theta = a$$
$$\tan\theta = \frac{b}{a}$$

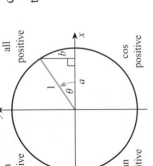

sin positive | all positive

tan positive | cos positive

$\tan\theta = h$

Trigonometrical ratios

θ	0°	30°	45°	60°	90°	180°
$\sin\theta$	0	$\frac{1}{2}$	$\frac{1}{\sqrt{2}}$	$\frac{\sqrt{3}}{2}$	1	0
$\cos\theta$	1	$\frac{\sqrt{3}}{2}$	$\frac{1}{\sqrt{2}}$	$\frac{1}{2}$	0	−1
$\tan\theta$	0	$\frac{1}{\sqrt{3}}$	1	$\sqrt{3}$	–	0

Trigonometry

Circular measure

2π radians $= 360°$

If an angle is given in terms of π it can be assumed to be in radians.

Arc length $s = r\theta$ (θ is in radians)

Area of sector $A = \frac{1}{2}r^2\theta$ (θ is in radians)

Small-angle approximations
B

$\sin\theta \approx \theta$ $\cos\theta \approx 1 - \dfrac{\theta^2}{2}$ $\tan\theta \approx \theta$ (θ is in radians)

Compound-angle formulae
B

$\sin(\theta \pm \varphi) = \sin\theta \cos\varphi \pm \cos\theta \sin\varphi$

$\cos(\theta \pm \varphi) = \cos\theta \cos\varphi \mp \sin\theta \sin\varphi$

$\tan(\theta \pm \varphi) = \dfrac{\tan\theta \pm \tan\varphi}{1 \mp \tan\theta \tan\varphi}$, where θ, φ and $(\theta \pm \varphi) \neq (k + \tfrac{1}{2})\pi$ (k is an integer)

The form $r\sin(\theta + \alpha)$, etc.
B

$a\cos\theta + b\sin\theta = r\cos(\theta - \alpha)$ where $r = \sqrt{a^2 + b^2}$, $\cos\alpha = \dfrac{a}{r}$ and $\sin\alpha = \dfrac{b}{r}$

$a\cos\theta + b\sin\theta = r\sin(\theta + \beta)$ where $r = \sqrt{a^2 + b^2}$, $\sin\beta = \dfrac{a}{r}$ and $\cos\beta = \dfrac{b}{r}$

Factor formulae
B

$\sin\theta \pm \sin\varphi = 2\sin\tfrac{1}{2}(\theta \pm \varphi)\cos\tfrac{1}{2}(\theta \mp \varphi)$

$\cos\theta + \cos\varphi = 2\cos\tfrac{1}{2}(\theta + \varphi)\cos\tfrac{1}{2}(\theta - \varphi)$

$\cos\theta - \cos\varphi = -2\sin\tfrac{1}{2}(\theta + \varphi)\sin\tfrac{1}{2}(\theta - \varphi)$

Double-angle formulae
B

$\sin 2\theta = 2\sin\theta\cos\theta$

$\tan 2\theta = \dfrac{2\tan\theta}{1 - \tan^2\theta}$

$\sin^2\theta = \tfrac{1}{2}(1 - \cos 2\theta)$

$\cos 2\theta = \begin{cases} 2\cos^2\theta - 1 \\ \cos^2\theta - \sin^2\theta \\ 1 - 2\sin^2\theta \end{cases}$

$\cos^2\theta = \tfrac{1}{2}(1 + \cos 2\theta)$

Half-angle formulae
E

For $t = \tan\tfrac{1}{2}\theta$: $\sin\theta = \dfrac{2t}{1 + t^2}$ $\cos\theta = \dfrac{1 - t^2}{1 + t^2}$ $\tan\theta = \dfrac{2t}{1 - t^2}$

Solution of trigonometrical equations
B

A trigonometrical equation can have an infinite number of roots (unless its domain is restricted or it has no roots).

For example, if $\sin\theta = \tfrac{1}{2}$ then $\theta = \ldots, -\dfrac{11\pi}{6}, -\dfrac{7\pi}{6}, \dfrac{\pi}{6}, \dfrac{5\pi}{6}, \ldots$.

In this case, $\dfrac{\pi}{6}$ is called the **principal value.**

Principal values

$-\dfrac{\pi}{2} \leqslant \arcsin x \leqslant \dfrac{\pi}{2}$ $0 \leqslant \arccos x \leqslant \pi$ $-\dfrac{\pi}{2} < \arctan x < \dfrac{\pi}{2}$

(The notation $\sin^{-1}x$ (etc.) is also widely used.)

General solutions of trigonometrical equations
E

In the following general solutions, p stands for the principal value of the relevant inverse trigonometrical function, solutions are given in radians and n is any integer.

Equation	General solution
$\sin\theta = c$	$\theta = 2n\pi + p$ and $\theta = (2n + 1)\pi - p$ or $\theta = n\pi + (-1)^n p$
$\cos\theta = c$	$\theta = 2n\pi \pm p$
$\tan\theta = c$	$\theta = n\pi + p$

Complex numbers

Notation and definitions

$i^2 = -1$ Alternative notation: $j^2 = -1$

i is most commonly used for $\sqrt{-1}$ by mathematicians; j is most commonly used by engineers.

Argand diagram

A point in two-dimensional space, using a real (Re) axis and an imaginary (Im) axis, represents the complex number.

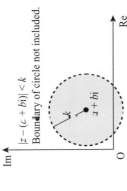

Cartesian form

$z = x + iy$ (The notation $z = x + jy$ is also used.)

$\text{Re}(z) = x; \quad \text{Im}(z) = y$

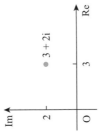

Polar (modulus argument) form

$r = \bmod z = |z| = \sqrt{x^2 + y^2}$

$\arg z = \theta$ where $\cos\theta = \dfrac{x}{|z|}$ and $\sin\theta = \dfrac{y}{|z|}$ and $-\pi < \theta \leqq \pi$

$\arg 0$ is undefined.

$z = [r, \theta] = r(\cos\theta + i\sin\theta) \quad \dfrac{1}{z} = \dfrac{1}{r}(\cos\theta - i\sin\theta)$

$z = r e^{i\theta}$ is the exponential form of the complex number.

Complex conjugate

Conjugate of z, $\quad z^* = x - iy$.

$\quad\quad \dfrac{1}{z} = \dfrac{x - iy}{x^2 + y^2} = \dfrac{z^*}{|z|^2}$ (The notation $\bar{z}$ is also used.)

$zz^* = |z|^2$ $z^* = r(\cos\theta - i\sin\theta)$

Adding and subtracting complex numbers

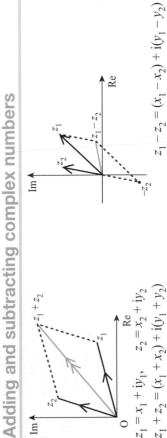

$z_1 = x_1 + iy_1, \quad z_2 = x_2 + iy_2$

$z_1 + z_2 = (x_1 + x_2) + i(y_1 + y_2)$

$z_1 - z_2 = (x_1 - x_2) + i(y_1 - y_2)$

Multiplying and dividing complex numbers in polar form

For $z_1 = r_1(\cos\theta_1 + i\sin\theta_1)$, $z_2 = r_2(\cos\theta_2 + i\sin\theta_2)$

$z_1 z_2 = r_1 r_2 (\cos(\theta_1 + \theta_2) + i\sin(\theta_1 + \theta_2))$

$\dfrac{z_1}{z_2} = \dfrac{r_1}{r_2}(\cos(\theta_1 - \theta_2) + i\sin(\theta_1 - \theta_2))$

$z = re^{i\theta}$ is the exponential form of the complex number

de Moivre's theorem

$\{r(\cos\theta + i\sin\theta)\}^n = r^n(\cos n\theta + i\sin n\theta)$ for n an integer (if n is rational, but not an integer, de Mcivre's theorem gives one of the possible values)

Euler's formulae

$e^{i\theta} = \cos\theta + i\sin\theta$

$e^{-i\theta} = \cos\theta - i\sin\theta$

consequently $e^{i\pi} + 1 = 0$

The roots of $z^n = 1$ are given by $z = \exp\left(\dfrac{2\pi k}{n}i\right)$ for $k = 0, 1, 2, \ldots, n-1$

If $z = e^{i\theta}$ then

$\cos\theta = \dfrac{1}{2}\left(z + \dfrac{1}{z}\right) \quad \sin\theta = \dfrac{1}{2i}\left(z - \dfrac{1}{z}\right)$

Loci

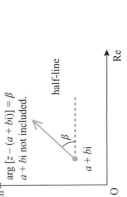

$|z - (a + bi)| = k$

$|z - (a + bi)| < k$
Boundary of circle not included.

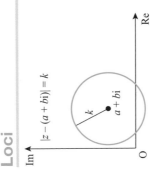

$\arg[z - (a + bi)] = \beta$
$a + bi$ not included.
half-line

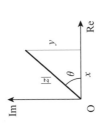

$|z - z_1| = |z - z_2|$
perpendicular bisector

Matrices

The null matrix

Also known as the **zero matrix**; all entries are zero.

The 2×2 null matrix is $\begin{pmatrix} 0 & 0 \\ 0 & 0 \end{pmatrix}$.

The identity matrix

Also known as the **unit matrix**, usually denoted by **I**.

The 2×2 identity matrix is $\begin{pmatrix} 1 & 0 \\ 0 & 1 \end{pmatrix}$. For any 2×2 matrix **M**: $\quad$ **IM = MI = M**.

Identity matrices are square.

The determinant of a 2 × 2 matrix

For $\mathbf{M} = \begin{pmatrix} a_1 & b_1 \\ a_2 & b_2 \end{pmatrix}$: $\quad \det\mathbf{M} = \begin{vmatrix} a_1 & b_1 \\ a_2 & b_2 \end{vmatrix} = a_1 b_2 - a_2 b_1.$

The determinant of a 3 × 3 matrix

For $\mathbf{M} = \begin{pmatrix} a_1 & b_1 & c_1 \\ a_2 & b_2 & c_2 \\ a_3 & b_3 & c_3 \end{pmatrix}$: $\quad \det\mathbf{M} = \begin{vmatrix} a_1 & b_1 & c_1 \\ a_2 & b_2 & c_2 \\ a_3 & b_3 & c_3 \end{vmatrix} = a_1 \begin{vmatrix} b_2 & c_2 \\ b_3 & c_3 \end{vmatrix} - b_1 \begin{vmatrix} a_2 & c_2 \\ a_3 & c_3 \end{vmatrix} + c_1 \begin{vmatrix} a_2 & b_2 \\ a_3 & b_3 \end{vmatrix}.$

Minors and cofactors

The minor of a_1 is obtained by crossing out the row and column containing a_1. The minor of a_1 is $\begin{vmatrix} b_2 & c_2 \\ b_3 & c_3 \end{vmatrix}$.

$$\begin{array}{|c|c|c|} \hline a_1 & b_1 & c_1 \\ \hline a_2 & b_2 & c_2 \\ a_3 & b_3 & c_3 \end{array}$$

The **cofactor** of a_1, denoted by A_1, is the minor of a_1, together with the correct sign, which can be obtained from this diagram: $\begin{vmatrix} + & - & + \\ - & + & - \\ + & - & + \end{vmatrix}$.

A determinant can be evaluated by multiplying the elements of any row (or column) by their cofactors and adding together the results.

The inverse and transpose of a matrix

The transpose of matrix **M** is the matrix whose rows are the columns of **M** and whose columns are the rows of **M**. It is denoted by $\mathbf{M}^\mathrm{T}$.

i.e. if $\mathbf{M} = \begin{pmatrix} a & c \\ b & d \end{pmatrix}$ then $\mathbf{M}^\mathrm{T} = \begin{pmatrix} a & b \\ c & d \end{pmatrix}$.

The inverse of a non-singular matrix

(The determinant of a singular matrix is zero and the matrix has no inverse.)
The inverse of matrix **M** is denoted by $\mathbf{M}^{-1}$.

The inverse of a 2 × 2 matrix

For $\mathbf{M} = \begin{pmatrix} a_1 & b_1 \\ a_2 & b_2 \end{pmatrix}$: $\quad \mathbf{M}^{-1} = \frac{1}{\det\mathbf{M}} \begin{pmatrix} b_2 & -b_1 \\ -a_2 & a_1 \end{pmatrix}$

The inverse of a 3 × 3 matrix

For $\mathbf{M} = \begin{pmatrix} a_1 & b_1 & c_1 \\ a_2 & b_2 & c_2 \\ a_3 & b_3 & c_3 \end{pmatrix}$: $\quad \mathbf{M}^{-1} = \frac{1}{\det\mathbf{M}} \begin{pmatrix} A_1 & B_1 & C_1 \\ A_2 & B_2 & C_2 \\ A_3 & B_3 & C_3 \end{pmatrix}^\mathrm{T} = \frac{1}{\det\mathbf{M}} \begin{pmatrix} A_1 & A_2 & A_3 \\ B_1 & B_2 & B_3 \\ C_1 & C_2 & C_3 \end{pmatrix}$

where A_1 is the cofactor of a_1, etc.

A matrix is said to be **symmetric** if it is the same as its transpose.

A matrix is said to be **orthogonal** if its inverse is the same as its transpose.

Simultaneous equations

$a_1 x + b_1 y = c_1$
$a_2 x + b_2 y = c_2$
$\quad$ can be written $\mathbf{M} \begin{pmatrix} x \\ y \end{pmatrix} = \begin{pmatrix} c_1 \\ c_2 \end{pmatrix}$, where $\mathbf{M} = \begin{pmatrix} a_1 & b_1 \\ a_2 & b_2 \end{pmatrix}$

and (if $\det\mathbf{M} \neq 0$) can be solved by $\begin{pmatrix} x \\ y \end{pmatrix} = \mathbf{M}^{-1} \begin{pmatrix} c_1 \\ c_2 \end{pmatrix}$.

A similar result applies for three equations in three unknowns (and beyond).

The inverse and transpose of a matrix product

$(\mathbf{AB})^{-1} = \mathbf{B}^{-1}\mathbf{A}^{-1} \qquad (\mathbf{AB})^\mathrm{T} = \mathbf{B}^\mathrm{T}\mathbf{A}^\mathrm{T}$

Matrices

Matrix transformations

Anticlockwise rotation through angle θ about centre O: $\begin{pmatrix} \cos\theta & -\sin\theta \\ \sin\theta & \cos\theta \end{pmatrix}$

Reflection in the line $y = x\tan\theta$: $\begin{pmatrix} \cos 2\theta & \sin 2\theta \\ \sin 2\theta & -\cos 2\theta \end{pmatrix}$

The matrix product $\mathbf{AB}$ represents the transformation that results from the transformation represented by $\mathbf{B}$ followed by the transformation represented by $\mathbf{A}$.

Invariant points and lines

A line is invariant under a given transformation if any point on the line before the transformation is still on the line after the transformation. For example, any line perpendicular to the mirror line is an invariant line for a reflection in two dimensions.

A point is invariant under a given transformation if it remains in the same place after the transformation. For example, the centre of rotation is an invariant point for a rotation in two dimensions.

Area and volume scale factors for transformations

For a transformation represented by a 2×2 matrix, the determinant of the matrix is the area scale factor of the transformation.

For a transformation represented by a 3×3 matrix, the determinant of the matrix is the volume scale factor of the transformation.

Diagonally dominant matrices

In every row of a diagonally dominant matrix, the modulus of the diagonal entry (the one in the 4th column of the 4th row, etc.) is larger than the sum of the moduli of all the other entries in that row.

Eigenvalues and eigenvectors

For matrix $\mathbf{M}$, if there is a non-zero vector, $\mathbf{s}$, such that $\mathbf{Ms} = \lambda\mathbf{s}$, for a scalar λ, then $\mathbf{s}$ is an eigenvector of the matrix and λ is its corresponding eigenvalue.

Eigenvalues can be found by solving the **characteristic equation** $\det(\mathbf{M} - \lambda\mathbf{I}) = 0$.

Cayley–Hamilton theorem

Every square matrix satisfies its own characteristic equation.

Reducing a matrix to diagonal form

If $\mathbf{S}$ is the matrix composed of eigenvectors of $\mathbf{M}$ as its columns and $\mathbf{S}$ is non-singular then $\mathbf{\Lambda} = \mathbf{S}^{-1}\mathbf{MS}$ where $\mathbf{\Lambda}$ is the matrix with the corresponding eigenvalues on its leading diagonal and zeros elsewhere.

So $\mathbf{M} = \mathbf{S}\mathbf{\Lambda}\mathbf{S}^{-1}$

and $\mathbf{M}^n = \mathbf{S}\mathbf{\Lambda}^n\mathbf{S}^{-1}$

Markov chains

A Markov chain is a sequence of events where the probability of an outcome (state) at one stage depends only on the outcome (state) at the previous stage.

Statistics usage	Pure mathematics usage
For $\mathbf{p}$ as a row vector	For $\mathbf{p}$ as a column vector
$\mathbf{p}_{n+1} = \mathbf{p}_n\mathbf{P}$	$\mathbf{p}_{n+1} = \mathbf{P}\mathbf{p}_n$
Long run proportion $\mathbf{p} = \mathbf{p}\mathbf{P}$	Long run proportion $\mathbf{p} = \mathbf{P}\mathbf{p}$

where $\mathbf{P}$ is the transition matrix.

Expected run length

If the probability of staying in a given state is α, the expected run length (i.e. the mean number of transitions with no change from the current state) is $\dfrac{\alpha}{1-\alpha}$.

In a periodic Markov chain, for some positive integer k, $\mathbf{P}^k = \mathbf{P}$ where $\mathbf{P}$ is the transition matrix. The period is $k - 1$.

A Markov chain has an absorbing state if, once it is in a particular state, it stays in it.

A Markov chain has a reflecting barrier if, once it is in a particular state, the next state has to occur.

Vectors

Notation

Vectors are either printed in bold, e.g. **r**, handwritten using underlining, or with an arrow, e.g. $\overrightarrow{AB}$.

A vector has **magnitude** (or modulus) and **direction**; these are often denoted by r and θ in two dimensions. A vector can be represented by a directed line segment with the direction of the line being the direction of the vector and the length of the line being proportional to the magnitude of the vector.

Unit vectors parallel to co-ordinate axes
In two dimensions **i**, **j**
In three dimensions **i**, **j**, **k**

A vector may be expressed in terms of these unit vectors,

e.g. $2\mathbf{i} + 3\mathbf{j}$, $3\mathbf{i} - \mathbf{j} + 4\mathbf{k}$, or as a column vector, e.g. $\begin{pmatrix} 2 \\ 3 \end{pmatrix}$, $\begin{pmatrix} 3 \\ -1 \\ 4 \end{pmatrix}$.

The point $P(x_1, y_1, z_1)$ has **position vector**

$$\overrightarrow{OP} = \mathbf{r} = x_1\mathbf{i} + y_1\mathbf{j} + z_1\mathbf{k} = \begin{pmatrix} x_1 \\ y_1 \\ z_1 \end{pmatrix}$$

The length of $\mathbf{r} = |\mathbf{r}| = \sqrt{x_1^2 + y_1^2 + z_1^2}$

The **unit vector** in the direction of $\mathbf{r}$ is $\hat{\mathbf{r}} = \dfrac{\mathbf{r}}{|\mathbf{r}|}$

Parallel vectors

$\begin{pmatrix} a_1 \\ a_2 \\ a_3 \end{pmatrix}$ is parallel to $\begin{pmatrix} ka_1 \\ ka_2 \\ ka_3 \end{pmatrix}$ For $k > 0$, the vectors have the same direction.

If $k < 0$, the vectors are in opposite directions.

The scalar product

$\mathbf{u}.\mathbf{v} = |\mathbf{u}||\mathbf{v}| \cos\theta = u_1v_1 + u_2v_2 + u_3v_3$

where $\mathbf{u} = \begin{pmatrix} u_1 \\ u_2 \\ u_3 \end{pmatrix}$ and $\mathbf{v} = \begin{pmatrix} v_1 \\ v_2 \\ v_3 \end{pmatrix}$

The **resolved part** of a vector $\mathbf{a}$ in the direction of $\mathbf{u}$ is $\dfrac{\mathbf{a}.\mathbf{u}}{|\mathbf{u}|}$

Perpendicular vectors
If $\mathbf{a}$ and $\mathbf{b}$ are non-zero vectors and $\mathbf{a}.\mathbf{b} = 0$, then $\mathbf{a}$ and $\mathbf{b}$ are perpendicular.

Lines

If A is the point with position vector $\mathbf{a} = a_1\mathbf{i} + a_2\mathbf{j} + a_3\mathbf{k}$ and the direction vector **u** is given by $\mathbf{u} = u_1\mathbf{i} + u_2\mathbf{j} + u_3\mathbf{k}$, then the equation of the straight line through A with direction vector **u** can be given as follows.

Vector form $\mathbf{r} = \mathbf{a} + t\mathbf{u}$ where **r** is the position vector of a point on the line

Component form $\begin{pmatrix} x \\ y \\ z \end{pmatrix} = \begin{pmatrix} a_1 \\ a_2 \\ a_3 \end{pmatrix} + t\begin{pmatrix} u_1 \\ u_2 \\ u_3 \end{pmatrix}$

Cartesian form $\dfrac{x - a_1}{u_1} = \dfrac{y - a_2}{u_2} = \dfrac{z - a_3}{u_3}\ (= t)$ where $u_1, u_2, u_3 \neq 0$

Any point on the line has co-ordinates $(a_1 + tu_1, a_2 + tu_2, a_3 + tu_3)$

If A has position vector $\mathbf{a}$ and B has position vector $\mathbf{b}$ then $\overrightarrow{AB} = \mathbf{b} - \mathbf{a}$

The line AB has vector equation $\mathbf{r} = \mathbf{a} + t(\mathbf{b} - \mathbf{a}) = (1 - t)\mathbf{a} + t\mathbf{b}$

The position vector of the point dividing AB in the ratio $\lambda : \mu$ is $\dfrac{\mu\mathbf{a} + \lambda\mathbf{b}}{\lambda + \mu}$

The position vector of the mid-point of AB is $\frac{1}{2}(\mathbf{a} + \mathbf{b})$

The length of AB is $\sqrt{(a_1 - b_1)^2 + (a_2 - b_2)^2 + (a_3 - b_3)^2}$

Planes

The equation of the plane with normal vector $\mathbf{n} = n_1\mathbf{i} + n_2\mathbf{j} + n_3\mathbf{k}$ through the point A, with position vector $\mathbf{a}$, can be given as follows.

Vector form $(\mathbf{r} - \mathbf{a}).\mathbf{n} = 0$ where **r** is the position vector of a point on the plane

Cartesian form $n_1x + n_2y + n_3z + d = 0$ where $d = -\mathbf{a}.\mathbf{n}$

The plane through non-collinear points A, B and C has vector equation
$\mathbf{r} = \mathbf{a} + s(\mathbf{b} - \mathbf{a}) + t(\mathbf{c} - \mathbf{a}) = (1 - s - t)\mathbf{a} + s\mathbf{b} + t\mathbf{c}$

The plane through A parallel to **u** and **v** (which are not parallel to each other) has equation $\mathbf{r} = \mathbf{a} + s\mathbf{u} + t\mathbf{v}$

A vector perpendicular to a plane is perpendicular to any line in the plane.

The angle between two planes equals the angle between their normals.

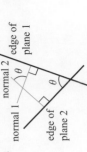

Vertices

Direction ratios and direction cosines

If α is the angle a straight line makes with the direction of the x axis, β with the y axis and γ with the z axis then its **direction cosines** are

$l = \cos\alpha$

$m = \cos\beta$

$n = \cos\gamma$

and $l^2 + m^2 + n^2 = 1$.

If $p : q : r = l : m : n$ then p, q, r are **direction ratios** for the straight line.

l, m and n are components of a *unit* direction vector for the line; p, q and r are components of any direction vector for the line.

Linear independence and dependence of vectors

If $\mathbf{a}_1$, $\mathbf{a}_2$, ..., $\mathbf{a}_n$ are vectors and it is possible to find scalars λ_1, λ_2, ..., λ_n which are not all zero such that $\lambda_1\mathbf{a}_1 + \lambda_2\mathbf{a}_2 + ... + \lambda_n\mathbf{a}_n = \mathbf{0}$ then the vectors are linearly dependent. Otherwise, they are linearly independent.

The distance of a point from a plane

The perpendicular distance of (a_1, a_2, a_3) from $n_1x + n_2y + n_3z + d = 0$ is

$$\frac{|n_1a_1 + n_2a_2 + n_3a_3 + d|}{\sqrt{n_1^2 + n_2^2 + n_3^2}}$$

Right-handed and left-handed sets of vectors

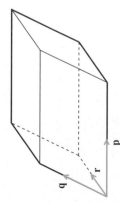

$\mathbf{p}$, $\mathbf{q}$, $\mathbf{r}$, in that order, are a left-handed set of vectors.

$\mathbf{a}$, $\mathbf{b}$, $\mathbf{c}$, in that order, are a right-handed set of vectors.

The usual axes, $x \to y \to z$, form a right-handed set of vectors. By contrast, $x \to y \to -z$ form a left-handed set.

The vector product

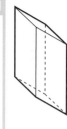

$$\mathbf{a} \times \mathbf{b} = |\mathbf{a}||\mathbf{b}|\sin\theta\,\hat{\mathbf{n}} = \begin{vmatrix} \mathbf{i} & a_1 & b_1 \\ \mathbf{j} & a_2 & b_2 \\ \mathbf{k} & a_3 & b_3 \end{vmatrix} = \begin{pmatrix} a_2b_3 - a_3b_2 \\ a_3b_1 - a_1b_3 \\ a_1b_2 - a_2b_1 \end{pmatrix}$$

The equation of a straight line using the vector product

The equation of the line through A with direction $\mathbf{u}$ is $(\mathbf{r} - \mathbf{a}) \times \mathbf{u} = \mathbf{0}$

Triple products

Scalar triple product
$$\mathbf{a}.(\mathbf{b} \times \mathbf{c}) = \begin{vmatrix} a_1 & b_1 & c_1 \\ a_2 & b_2 & c_2 \\ a_3 & b_3 & c_3 \end{vmatrix} = \mathbf{b}.(\mathbf{c} \times \mathbf{a}) = \mathbf{c}.(\mathbf{a} \times \mathbf{b})$$

The scalar triple product will be positive if $\mathbf{a}$, $\mathbf{b}$ and $\mathbf{c}$, in that order, form a right-handed set of vectors and negative if they form a left-handed set.

Vector triple product
$$\mathbf{a} \times (\mathbf{b} \times \mathbf{c}) = (\mathbf{a}.\mathbf{c})\mathbf{b} - (\mathbf{a}.\mathbf{b})\mathbf{c}$$

The shortest distance between two skew lines

Skew lines, in three dimensions, are not parallel and do not cross.
The shortest distance between the skew lines $\mathbf{r} = \mathbf{a} + \lambda\mathbf{d}$ and $\mathbf{r} = \mathbf{b} + \mu\mathbf{e}$ is

$$\left| (\mathbf{a} - \mathbf{b}).\frac{(\mathbf{d} \times \mathbf{e})}{|\mathbf{d} \times \mathbf{e}|} \right|$$

Volumes

A parallelepiped is a three-dimensional solid with six plane faces which occur in parallel pairs.

The volume of a parallelepiped with edges given by $\mathbf{a}$, $\mathbf{b}$, $\mathbf{c}$ is $|\mathbf{a}.(\mathbf{b} \times \mathbf{c})|$

A tetrahedron is a three-dimensional solid with four vertices.

The volume of tetrahedron OABC is $\frac{1}{6}|\mathbf{a}.(\mathbf{b} \times \mathbf{c})|$

Abstract algebra

Binary operations

A rule of combination which takes two elements of a set and combines them in some way to give a definite result is called a **binary operation**. Many binary operations are denoted by conventional symbols such as $+$ or $\times$, but other symbols such as $*$ and $\bullet$ can be used, so that $x \bullet y$, for example, means the result of combining x and y. Familiar binary operations on the set of real numbers include addition, subtraction, multiplication and division.

Some definitions of a binary operation require that it is also closed (see below).

Associative
A binary operation, represented by the symbol $*$, is associative if $(x * y) * z = x * (y * z)$ for all possible elements x, y and z; in this case, $x * y * z$ can be written without causing confusion. Addition of numbers is associative but subtraction is not since, for example, $(5 - 2) - 1 \neq 5 - (2 - 1)$.

Closed
If the result of the binary operation combining any two elements in the set is always in the set, the set is said to be closed under the operation.

Commutative
A binary operation is commutative if, for any two elements, combining them either way round gives the same result. Addition over the set of real numbers is commutative: $x + y = y + x$ for any pair of numbers x and y. Subtraction over the set of real numbers is not commutative: $x - y \neq y - x$ (for $x \neq y$).

Identity
For the binary operation $*$, an element e is said to be the identity element if it has the property that $x * e = e * x = x$ for all elements x. It can be shown that if an identity element exists for a particular binary operation on a set then the identity element is unique. 1 is the identity for multiplication over the set of real numbers; 0 is the identity for addition over the set of real numbers.

Inverse
The inverse element to x, denoted by x^{-1}, is such that $x * x^{-1} = x^{-1} * x = e$, where e is the identity element. Some elements may not have an inverse.

Distributive
For the two binary operations $*$ and $\bullet$ on a set of elements, the operation $*$ is distributive over the operation $\bullet$ if $a * (b \bullet c) = (a * b) \bullet (a * c)$ and $(b \bullet c) * a = (b * a) \bullet (c * a)$

Groups

A **group** $(S, \bullet)$ is a non-empty set S with a binary operation $\bullet$ and the following properties (the **group axioms**). Sometimes it is clear what the binary operation is, in which case the group could be denoted by a single letter, for example G.

1 S is closed under $\bullet$

2 $\bullet$ is associative.

3 There is an identity element in S.

4 Each element of S has an inverse in S.

A group which is also commutative is called **Abelian**.

A **subgroup** of $(S, \bullet)$ is a non-empty subset of S which forms a group under the same binary operation, $\bullet$

A **proper subgroup** of S is not identical to the original group.

The **order of a group** is the number of elements in its set, unless that set is infinite (in which case, the group is said to be an infinite group).

The **order of an element** is the least integer k such that $x^k = e$, where e is the identity element, and $x \bullet x = x^2$, etc. for the binary operation $\bullet$

Lagrange's theorem states that the order of any subgroup is a factor of the order of the group (for finite groups).

Cyclic group A finite group of order n with binary operation $\bullet$ is said to be **cyclic** if at least one of its elements, x, can be used to **generate** the group; this means that the elements x, x^2 (i.e. $x \bullet x$), x^3, ..., x^n are all different and so are the n elements in the group. A property of a cyclic group of order n is that for any generator x, $x^n = e$.

Isomorphic groups have the same structure as each other; there is a one-to-one mapping, f, from the elements of one group to the elements of the other group such that $f(x * y) = f(x) \bullet f(y)$ for all elements x, y, where $*$ and $\bullet$ are the respective binary operations in the groups.

Numerical methods

The numerical solution of equations

B, E

Change of sign methods such as decimal search, interval bisection and linear interpolation depend on the following.

If $f(b) > 0$ and $f(c) < 0$ for a continuous function $f(x)$ then $f(a) = 0$ for some value of a between b and c.

Newton–Raphson formula for solving $f(x) = 0$: $x_{r+1} = x_r - \dfrac{f(x_r)}{f'(x_r)}$

Fixed-point method

The **iteration** $x_{r+1} = g(x_r)$ will converge to a root, a, of the equation $x = g(x)$, given a suitable starting point, if $|g'(a)| < 1$

Cobweb and staircase diagrams

The cobweb diagram below shows convergence for solving $x = g(x)$ using the iteration $x_{r+1} = g(x_r)$.

The staircase diagram below shows convergence for finding one root of $x = g(x)$ using the iteration $x_{r+1} = g(x_r)$.

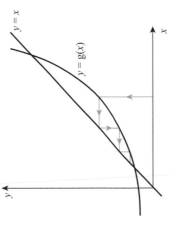

Secant method

For x_0, x_1 initial approximations to a root of $f(x) = 0$: $x_{r+1} = \dfrac{x_{r-1} f(x_r) - x_r f(x_{r-1})}{f(x_r) - f(x_{r-1})}$

Method of false position

If a root of $f(x) = 0$ lies between a and b then $c = \dfrac{af(b) - bf(a)}{f(b) - f(a)}$ gives an approximation of the root. The process can be repeated to get better approximations.

Taylor polynomials

E

$$f(a + h) = f(a) + hf'(a) + \frac{h^2}{2!}f''(a) + \text{error}$$

$$f(a + h) = f(a) + hf'(a) + \frac{h^2}{2!}f''(a + \xi), \quad 0 < \xi < h$$

$$f(x) = f(a) + (x - a)f'(a) + \frac{(x - a)^2}{2!}f''(a) + \text{error}$$

$$f(x) = f(a) + (x - a)f'(a) + \frac{(x - a)^2}{2!}f''(\eta), \quad a < \eta < x \ \ (\text{See also page 13.})$$

Error in a function

E

Error in $f(x) \approx (\text{error in } x) \times f'(x)$

Absolute and relative error

If X is an approximation to the exact value x, then

Absolute error $= X - x$

or Absolute error $= |X - x|$ with $X - x$ being described as 'error'

(There is no universally agreed usage of the term 'absolute error'.)

Relative error $= \dfrac{X - x}{x}$ (if $x \neq 0$); hence $X = x(1 + r)$ where r is the relative error

The **order** of an error refers to how an error is related to the 'step length' or 'strip length' in methods which involve such things. First-order error means that the error is proportional to the step/strip length. Second-order error means that the error is proportional to the square of the step/strip lengths and so on.

Convergence and errors

E

For an iteration of the form $x_{r+1} = f(x_r)$, which converges to α, successive small errors e_n are such that:

- if $f'(\alpha) \neq 0$, $e_{r+1} \approx f'(\alpha)e_r$. (This is first-order convergence.)
- if $f'(\alpha) = 0$, $e_{r+1} \approx ke_r^2$, (in general), where k is a constant. (This is second-order convergence.)

The **order of convergence** refers to how an error is related to the previous error in an iterative process. If the error is approximately proportional to the previous error, the convergence is first order; if it is approximately proportional to the square of the previous error, the convergence is second order.

Numerical methods

Approximations to functions [E]

Newton's forward difference interpolation formula

$$f(x) = f(x_0) + \frac{(x-x_0)}{h}\Delta f(x_0) + \frac{(x-x_0)(x-x_1)}{2!h^2}\Delta^2 f(x_0) + \ldots$$

where $\Delta f_0 = f_1 - f_0$, $\Delta^2 f_0 = \Delta f_1 - \Delta f_0$ and $f_0 = f(x_0)$, etc.

Lagrange's interpolation polynomial (or formula)

$$P_n(x) = \sum_{r=0}^{n} L_r(x)f(x_r), \text{ where } L_r(x) = \prod_{\substack{i=0 \\ i \neq r}}^{n}\left(\frac{x-x_i}{x_r-x_i}\right)$$

Newton's divided difference interpolation formula

$$f(x) = f[x_0] + (x-x_0)f[x_0,x_1] + (x-x_0)(x-x_1)f[x_0,x_1,x_2] + \ldots$$

where $f[x_0,x_1] = \dfrac{f(x_1)-f(x_0)}{x_1-x_0}$, $f[x_0,x_1,x_2] = \dfrac{f[x_1,x_2]-f[x_0,x_1]}{x_2-x_0}$, etc.

Numerical integration [A, B, E]

The trapezium rule

$$\int_a^b y\,dx \approx \tfrac{1}{2}h\{(y_0+y_n)+2(y_1+y_2+\ldots+y_{n-1})\} = T_n, \text{ where } h = \frac{b-a}{n} \text{ (second order)*}$$

The mid-point (or mid-ordinate) rule

$$\int_a^b y\,dx \approx h\{y_{\frac{1}{2}} + y_{1\frac{1}{2}} + \ldots + y_{n-1\frac{1}{2}} + y_{n-\frac{1}{2}}\} = M_n, \text{ where } h = \frac{b-a}{n} \text{ (second order)*}$$

Simpson's rule

For n even, where $h = \dfrac{b-a}{n}$,

$$\int_a^b y\,dx \approx \tfrac{1}{3}h\{(y_0+y_n)+4(y_1+y_3+\ldots+y_{n-1})+2(y_2+y_4+\ldots+y_{n-2})\} = S_n$$
$$\text{(fourth order)*}$$

Relationships between methods

If M_n denotes the result of using the mid-point rule with n strips, T_n denotes the result of using the trapezium rule with n strips and S_{2n} denotes the result of using Simpson's rule with $2n$ strips then

$$T_{2n} = \tfrac{1}{2}(M_n + T_n) \quad \text{and} \quad S_{2n} = \tfrac{1}{3}(2M_n + T_n) = \tfrac{1}{3}(4T_{2n} - T_n).$$

(The notation S_n needs to be treated with caution. Sometimes, as above, it means that there are n strips but, in more advanced use, it refers to n applications of the method and, hence, $2n$ strips.)

* refers to the order of error.

Numerical differentiation [E]

Forward difference $\quad f'(x) \approx \dfrac{f(x+h)-f(x)}{h}$ (first order)*

Central difference $\quad f'(x) \approx \dfrac{f(x+h)-f(x-h)}{2h}$ (second order)*

$$f''(x) \approx \frac{f(x+h)-2f(x)+f(x-h)}{h^2}$$

The Gaussian two-point integration rule

$$\int_{-h}^{h} f(x)\,dx \approx h\left[f\left(\frac{-h}{\sqrt{3}}\right) + f\left(\frac{h}{\sqrt{3}}\right)\right] \text{ (fourth order)*}$$

Numerical solution of first-order differential equations [E]

For $\dfrac{dy}{dx} = f(x,y)$ with initial conditions $x = x_0, y = y_0$

Euler's method

$$y_{r+1} = y_r + hf(x_r, y_r), \quad x_{r+1} = x_r + h$$

Runge–Kutta method, order 2 (modified Euler method)

$$y_{r+1} = y_r + \tfrac{1}{2}(k_1 + k_2), \quad x_{r+1} = x_r + h$$

where $k_1 = hf(x_r, y_r)$

$\qquad k_2 = hf(x_r + h, y_r + k_1)$

Runge–Kutta method, order 4

$$y_{r+1} = y_r + \tfrac{1}{6}(k_1 + 2k_2 + 2k_3 + k_4)$$

where $k_1 = hf(x_r, y_r)$

$\qquad k_2 = hf(x_r + \tfrac{1}{2}h, y_r + \tfrac{1}{2}k_1)$

$\qquad k_3 = hf(x_r + \tfrac{1}{2}h, y_r + \tfrac{1}{2}k_2)$

$\qquad k_4 = hf(x_r + h, y_r + k_3)$

* refers to the order of error.

Mechanics

Modelling terms

Freely jointed — If two rods are freely jointed, there is negligible friction at the join and they are free to rotate.

Inextensible — An inextensible string (or rod) cannot be stretched.

Lamina — A lamina is a two-dimensional shape with negligible thickness.

Light — A light body has negligible **weight**. Its mass can also be neglected.

Negligible — Small enough to ignore in the context.

Particle — A particle has mass but negligible size.

Rigid body — A rigid body stays the same shape whatever forces act on it.

Rod — A rod is a rigid one-dimensional body with negligible width and thickness; only the length matters.

Smooth — Friction should be ignored.

Thin — Has negligible thickness.

Uniform — The same throughout.

Scalars

Distance
Speed
Magnitude of acceleration
Energy, Work
Power
Mass

Vectors

Displacement
Velocity
Acceleration

Weight
Momentum, Impulse
Force

(See also page 24.)
A vector may be **resolved** into components in two perpendicular directions.

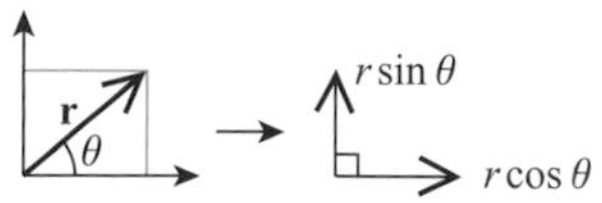

When two or more vectors are added, their **resultant** is obtained.

The diagram shows the resultant, **r**, of the vectors **a**, **b** and **c** (represented as directed line segments). When the resultant is zero, the directed line segments form a polygon. A special case of this is the triangle of forces: if a body is in equilibrium under the action of three forces, their lines of action are concurrent and the forces can be represented by directed line segments forming a triangle.

$r\sin\theta$
$r\cos\theta$
$\mathbf{r} = \mathbf{a} + \mathbf{b} + \mathbf{c}$

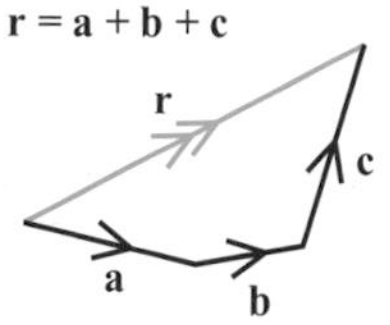

Kinematics

Constant acceleration formulae

$$\mathbf{s} = \mathbf{u}t + \tfrac{1}{2}\mathbf{a}t^2 \qquad \mathbf{s} = \tfrac{1}{2}(\mathbf{u}+\mathbf{v})t \qquad \mathbf{s} = \mathbf{v}t - \tfrac{1}{2}\mathbf{a}t^2$$
$$\mathbf{v} = \mathbf{u} + \mathbf{a}t \qquad \mathbf{v}^2 = \mathbf{u}^2 + 2\mathbf{a}.\mathbf{s} \qquad v^2 = u^2 + 2as \text{ (linear motion)}$$

Projectiles

$$a_x = \ddot{x} = \frac{d^2x}{dt^2} = 0 \qquad a_y = \ddot{y} = \frac{d^2y}{dt^2} = -g$$
$$v_x = \dot{x} = \frac{dx}{dt} = u\cos\alpha \qquad v_y = \dot{y} = \frac{dy}{dt} = u\sin\alpha - gt$$
$$x = ut\cos\alpha \qquad y = ut\sin\alpha - \tfrac{1}{2}gt^2$$

Equation of trajectory $\quad y = x\tan\alpha - \dfrac{gx^2}{2u^2\cos^2\alpha}$

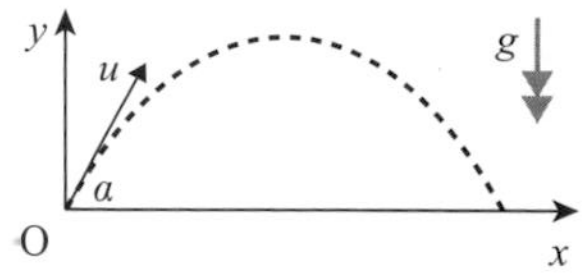

Initial velocity is u at angle α to the horizontal

Displacement, velocity and acceleration

$$\mathbf{v} = \frac{d\mathbf{s}}{dt} = \dot{\mathbf{s}}, \quad \mathbf{s} = \int \mathbf{v}\,dt, \qquad \mathbf{a} = \frac{d\mathbf{v}}{dt} = \dot{\mathbf{v}} = \frac{d^2\mathbf{s}}{dt^2} = \ddot{\mathbf{s}}, \quad \mathbf{v} = \int \mathbf{a}\,dt$$
$$v = \frac{ds}{dt} \qquad a = \frac{dv}{dt} = \frac{d^2s}{dt^2} \qquad a = v\frac{dv}{ds}$$

Displacement and position
The symbol **s** is often used for displacement, with **r** being used for the position vector (i.e. displacement from the origin).

Displacement, distance, velocity, speed
The displacement is the vector from the starting position to the current position. If a car is driven from its garage to the shops and then back to its garage, the displacement is zero but the distance travelled is the distance recorded on the car's milometer.

Velocity is a vector quantity; it includes the direction of travel. The speed is the magnitude of the velocity. A particle travelling in a circle at constant speed is changing its velocity because it is changing its direction of travel.

Relative position and relative velocity
The position vector of one point P may be given as the displacement from another point Q. This is called the **relative position** of P from Q. Note that both points may be moving.

Relative velocity is the derivative of the relative position. If P is travelling with a velocity $\mathbf{v}_P$ and Q is travelling with a velocity $\mathbf{v}_Q$ then the velocity of P relative to Q is $\mathbf{v}_P - \mathbf{v}_Q$.

Mechanics

Newton's laws of motion

1 Every particle continues in a state of rest or uniform motion in a straight line unless acted on by a resultant external force.

If the resultant of all the forces is zero, the particle has uniform velocity (which may be zero). If the resultant is not zero, the particle accelerates according to Newton's second law.

2 The rate of change of the linear momentum of a particle is proportional to the resultant force and is in the direction of the force. In the general case, using S.I. units, this is $\mathbf{F} = \dfrac{d}{dt}(m\mathbf{v})$.

When the mass is constant, the law becomes $\mathbf{F} = m\mathbf{a}$.

3 When one object exerts a force on another there is always a reaction which is equal, and opposite in direction, to the acting force.

In the case of two bodies, A and B, in contact, the force exerted by A on B is equal in magnitude to that exerted by B on A and is in the opposite direction.

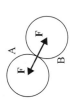

Equilibrium

A particle is in equilibrium if, and only if, there is no resultant force acting on it.

If a rigid body is in equilibrium, there is no resultant force and no resultant moment about any point. If the resultant force is zero then it is sufficient to find a single point about which all the (external) forces acting on the body have zero moment for the rigid body to be in equilibrium.

Lami's theorem

If a body is in equilibrium under the action of three (concurrent) forces, **A**, **B** and **C**, with lines of action at angles as shown then

$$\frac{A}{\sin \alpha} = \frac{B}{\sin \beta} = \frac{C}{\sin \gamma}.$$

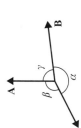

Types of force

Conservative	If a conservative force acts on a system, the total mechanical energy of the system (kinetic plus potential) is conserved.
Dissipative	If a dissipative force acts on a system, mechanical energy is lost by the system.
Normal reaction	The component of the reaction between two surfaces which is at right angles to the surfaces at the point of contact.
Tension	A pulling force (e.g. in a string or rod).
Thrust	A compression force.
Weight	The force of gravity acting on a body. The magnitude of the weight is mg where m is the mass of the object and $\mathbf{g}$ is the acceleration due to gravity.

Friction

Friction acts to oppose or prevent one surface from sliding over another.

$F = \mu R$ for dynamic friction, when sliding takes place.
$F \leqslant \mu R$ for static friction, when no sliding takes place.
μ is the **coefficient of friction**.

Limiting friction $F = \mu R$

Moment

The moment of the force, **F**, about an axis through A perpendicular to the plane containing A and **F**, is Fd. The moment can also be calculated by first resolving the force into components.

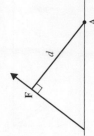

The moment of a force, **F**, about the origin, is $\mathbf{r} \times \mathbf{F}$ where **r** is the position vector of a point on the line of action of the force.

Couple

A couple is represented by two equal parallel forces not in the same line that are in opposite directions. This system has zero **resultant force** and an equal non-zero **moment** about any point. If the force has magnitude F and the distance apart of the lines of action is d then the moment of the couple is Fd. A couple has a **sense** that is usually referred to as **clockwise** or **anticlockwise**.

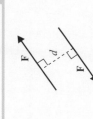

Mechanics

Momentum

C

Momentum is mv where m is the mass of the body and $\mathbf{v}$ is its velocity.

Impulse

C, D

Impulse is $\mathbf{F}t$ (for constant $\mathbf{F}$)

Impulse is the change in momentum, that is $m\mathbf{v} - m\mathbf{u}$

Impulse is $\int \mathbf{F}\,dt$ (for variable force)

Impacts

C

Conservation of momentum

$m_1u_1 + m_2u_2 = m_1v_1 + m_2v_2$

Newton's experimental law (sometimes called Newton's law of impact)

$$v_2 - v_1 = -e(u_2 - u_1)$$

where e is the **coefficient of restitution**.

$$e = \frac{\text{velocity of separation}}{\text{velocity of approach}} = \frac{v_2 - v_1}{u_1 - u_2}$$

For an **inelastic collision**, $e = 0$.

For a **perfectly elastic collision**, $e = 1$ and K.E. is conserved in this case.

Oblique impact is not direct, it is at an angle.

If two (or more) particles **coalesce**, they combine and become one particle.

Before

m_1 u_1 m_2 u_2

After

m_1 v_1 m_2 v_2

Work, energy and power

C, E

The work–energy principle

The total **mechanical** work done by the forces acting on a body is equal to the increase in the kinetic energy of the body.

Work done by a constant force is $W = F(s\cos\theta)$

$\qquad\qquad\qquad\qquad\qquad = (F\cos\theta)s$

θ F s

The work done by force $\mathbf{F}$ when a body is displaced by $\mathbf{s}$ is $\mathbf{F}\cdot\mathbf{s}$.

Kinetic energy (K.E.) is $\frac{1}{2}mv^2$.

Work done against gravity is called gravitational potential energy (G.P.E.) and is mgh.

Power is $\dfrac{dW}{dt} = Fv\cos\theta$

Variable force

Work done by the force is $\int F\,ds$ (one dimension)   Work is $\int \mathbf{F}\cdot\mathbf{ds}$ (vector form)

Power of the force is $P = Fv$ (one dimension)   Power is $\mathbf{F}\cdot\mathbf{v}$ (vector form)

Energy increase is $\int P\,dt$

Elastic strings and springs

E

Hooke's law

$T = kx$ where k is the stiffness

$T = \dfrac{\lambda}{l_0}x$ where λ is the modulus of elasticity and l_0 is the natural length

Energy stored, called elastic potential energy (E.P.E.), is $\frac{1}{2}kx^2 = \frac{1}{2}\dfrac{\lambda}{l_0}x^2$

Potential energy at equilibrium

E

If a particle is acted on by conservative forces only, and its potential energy can be expressed in terms of a single variable, the equilibrium positions are where its potential energy has a stationary value. Its P.E. has a maximum at a position of unstable equilibrium and a minimum at a position of stable equilibrium.

Note that potential energy is the energy which a body has as a result of its position. This includes gravitational potential energy and elastic potential energy.

Types of equilibrium

E

Neutral   If a body is resting in neutral equilibrium and is displaced a small amount from the equilibrium position, it will be in another, similar, position of equilibrium. For example, a cylinder resting on its curved surface on a horizontal plane.

Stable   If a body is resting in stable equilibrium and is displaced a small amount from the equilibrium position, it will return to its equilibrium position. For example, a cylinder resting on its circular face on a horizontal plane returns to its original position when it is tipped slightly so that the circular faces are no longer horizontal.

Unstable   If a body is resting in unstable equilibrium and is displaced a small amount from the equilibrium position, it will not return to its equilibrium position. For example, a pencil resting on its point.

Mechanics

C Centre of mass

$$\left(\sum m\right)\bar{x} = \sum(mx) \qquad \left(\sum m\right)\bar{\mathbf{r}} = \sum(m\mathbf{r})$$

Uniform body (angles in radians)	Centre of mass
Triangular lamina	$\frac{2}{3}$ along the median from the vertex
Solid hemisphere of radius r	$\frac{3}{8}r$ from the centre
Hemispherical shell of radius r	$\frac{1}{2}r$ from the centre
Solid cone or pyramid of height h	$\frac{1}{4}h$ above the base on the line from the centre of the base to the vertex
Sector of a circle of radius r with an angle of 2θ at the centre	$\dfrac{2r\sin\theta}{3\theta}$ from the centre
Arc of a circle of radius r with an angle of 2θ at the centre	$\dfrac{r\sin\theta}{\theta}$ from the centre
Conical shell of height h	$\frac{1}{3}h$ above the base on the line from the centre of the base to the vertex
Wire in the form of a semi-circle of radius r	$\dfrac{2r}{\pi}$ from the centre
Semi-circular lamina of radius r	$\dfrac{4r}{3\pi}$ from the centre

E Laminae and solids of revolution

Laminae

$$\left(\int_a^b y\, dx\right)\bar{x} = \int_a^b xy\, dx, \qquad \left(\int_a^b y\, dx\right)\bar{y} = \int_a^b \tfrac{1}{2}y^2\, dx$$

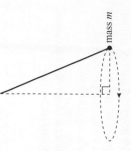

Solids of revolution about the x axis

$$\left(\int_a^b \pi y^2\, dx\right)\bar{x} = \int_a^b \pi xy^2\, dx, \qquad \bar{y} = 0$$

Solids of revolution about the y axis

$$\bar{x} = 0, \qquad \left(\int_p^q \pi x^2\, dy\right)\bar{y} = \int_p^q \pi x^2 y\, dy$$

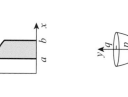

C, D Circular motion

Angular velocity
$$\omega = \dot{\theta}$$

Radial velocity
$$\dot{r} = 0 \quad (r \text{ is a constant})$$

Transverse (tangential) velocity
$$v = r\dot{\theta} = r\omega$$

Radial acceleration
$$-r\omega^2 = -r\dot{\theta}^2 = \frac{-v^2}{r}$$

Transverse (tangential) acceleration
$$\dot{v} = r\ddot{\theta}$$

Banking
Inclination of a surface to the horizontal, especially of a road or a train track round a corner.

Camber
The slope of a road from its centre to its edge.

Conical pendulum
A particle attached to a string (or rod) moves in a horizontal circle with the centre of the circle below the point of attachment of the string (or rod).

E Rotation with constant angular acceleration (α)

Rotation through angle θ, increasing from angular speed ω_0 to ω_1:

$$\theta = \omega_0 t + \tfrac{1}{2}\alpha t^2 \qquad \theta = \tfrac{1}{2}(\omega_0 + \omega_1)t \qquad \theta = \omega_1 t - \tfrac{1}{2}\alpha t^2$$

$$\omega_1 = \omega_0 + \alpha t \qquad \omega_1^2 = \omega_0^2 + 2\alpha\theta$$

E Radial, transverse and tangential directions

The radial direction is along the position vector, away from the origin.

The transverse direction is perpendicular to the position vector, in the sense of θ increasing.

The tangential direction is parallel to the instantaneous direction of motion, i.e. parallel to the velocity vector.

Mechanics

Rotation about a fixed axis and moments of inertia　E

Moment of inertia

$$I = \sum mr^2$$

For a force with moment C about the axis and angular displacement θ:

$C = I\ddot\theta$ 　　Kinetic energy is $\frac{1}{2}I\dot\theta^2$ 　　Work done is $\int C\, d\theta$

Angular momentum $I\omega = I\dot\theta$

Angular momentum is conserved if there is no resultant moment about the axis of rotation.

Uniform body of mass M	**Moment of inertia**
Thin rod, length $2l$, about perpendicular axis through the centre	$\frac{1}{3}Ml^2$
Rectangular lamina about axis in plane bisecting edges of length $2l$	$\frac{1}{3}Ml^2$
Thin rod, length $2l$, about perpendicular axis through end	$\frac{4}{3}Ml^2$
Rectangular lamina about edge perpendicular to edges of length $2l$	$\frac{4}{3}Ml^2$
Rectangular lamina, sides $2a$ and $2b$, about perpendicular axis through centre	$\frac{1}{3}M(a^2 + b^2)$
Hoop or cylindrical shell of radius r about perpendicular axis through centre	Mr^2
Hoop of radius r about a diameter	$\frac{1}{2}Mr^2$
Disc or solid cylinder of radius r about axis	$\frac{1}{2}Mr^2$
Disc of radius r about a diameter	$\frac{1}{4}Mr^2$
Solid sphere of radius r about a diameter	$\frac{2}{5}Mr^2$
Spherical shell of radius r about a diameter	$\frac{2}{3}Mr^2$

Parallel axes theorem

$$I_A = I_G + M(AG)^2$$

where I_G is the moment of inertia about an axis through the centre of mass, G; I_A is the moment of inertia about a parallel axis through point A and AG is the distance between the axes.

Perpendicular axes theorem

$$I_z = I_x + I_y \quad \text{(for a lamina in the } (x, y) \text{ plane)}$$

Radius of gyration

If the moment of inertia of a body about an axis is written as Mk^2 then the radius of gyration about the axis is said to be k.

General motion in a plane using polar co-ordinates

Radial velocity

$\dot r$

Transverse velocity

$r\dot\theta$

Radial acceleration

$\ddot r - r\dot\theta^2$

Transverse acceleration

$$r\ddot\theta + 2\dot r\dot\theta = \frac{1}{r}\frac{d(r^2\dot\theta)}{dt}$$

Period of oscillations of a simple pendulum　E

A simple pendulum is a particle on a light, inextensible string (or a light rod); it swings backwards and forwards in a vertical plane.

$$T = 2\pi\sqrt{\frac{l}{g}}$$

Period of small oscillations of a compound pendulum　E

A compound pendulum is a rigid body which can rotate about a fixed horizontal axis.

$$T = 2\pi\sqrt{\frac{I}{mgh}}$$

Periodic motion　E

The motion of a **particle** is periodic if the displacement, velocity and acceleration are **periodic functions** of time. The period is the time taken for one full cycle.

Oscillations about a position of stable equilibrium　E

For small oscillations about a position of stable equilibrium, often the period can be found by differentiating the energy equation and comparing the result to the SHM equation $\ddot x = -\omega^2 x$; the period is $\frac{2\pi}{\omega}$.

Mechanics

Quantity	Formula	Dimensions	SI unit
Area	lw	L^2	m^2
Volume	lwh	L^3	m^3
Speed	d/t	LT^{-1}	ms^{-1}
Acceleration	v/t	LT^{-2}	ms^{-2}
Acceleration due to gravity, g	–	LT^{-2}	ms^{-2}
Force	$F = ma$	MLT^{-2}	N, newton
Weight	mg	MLT^{-2}	N, newton
Kinetic energy	$\frac{1}{2}mv^2$	ML^2T^{-2}	J, joule
Gravitational potential energy	mgh	ML^2T^{-2}	J, joule
Work	Fs	ML^2T^{-2}	J, joule
Power	Fv	ML^2T^{-3}	W, watt
Impulse	Ft	MLT^{-1}	Ns
Momentum	mv	MLT^{-1}	Ns
Pressure	Force/Area	$ML^{-1}T^{-2}$	Nm^{-2}, pascal
Density	m/V	ML^{-3}	kgm^{-3}
Moment	Fd	ML^2T^{-2}	Nm
Angle θ	$s = r\theta$	Dimensionless	(radian)
Angular velocity	$\dfrac{\text{Angle}}{\text{Time}}$	T^{-1}	$rad\,s^{-1}$
Angular acceleration	$\dfrac{\text{Angular velocity}}{\text{Time}}$	T^{-2}	$rad\,s^{-2}$
Young's modulus, E	$T = \dfrac{EA}{l_0}x$	$ML^{-1}T^{-2}$	Nm^{-2}, pascal
Modulus of elasticity, λ	$T = \lambda x/l_0$	MLT^{-2}	N
Stiffness, k	$T = kx$	MT^{-2}	Nm^{-1}
Gravitational constant, G	$F = \dfrac{Gm_1m_2}{d^2}$	$M^{-1}L^3T^{-2}$	Nm^2kg^{-2}
Period	Time interval	T	s
Frequency	$\dfrac{1}{\text{Period}}$	T^{-1}	Hz, hertz
Coefficient of restitution, e	$\dfrac{V \text{ separation}}{V \text{ approach}}$	Dimensionless	–
Coefficient of friction, μ	$F = \mu R$	Dimensionless	–
Moment of inertia	$\sum mr^2$	ML^2	kgm^2

Oscillations

Simple harmonic motion (SHM)

$$\frac{d^2x}{dt^2} + \omega^2x = 0 \text{ or } \ddot{x} = -\omega^2x$$

$$x = A\sin\omega t + B\cos\omega t = a\sin(\omega t + \varepsilon) = a\cos(\omega t - \varphi)$$

where $a = \sqrt{A^2 + B^2}$, $\sin\varepsilon = \dfrac{B}{a}$, $\cos\varepsilon = \dfrac{A}{a}$, $\sin\varphi = \dfrac{A}{a}$ and $\cos\varphi = \dfrac{B}{a}$

The speed, v, is given by $v^2 = \omega^2(a^2 - x^2)$

The period is $T = \dfrac{2\pi}{\omega}$

The **amplitude** (a) is the maximum distance from the central (equilibrium) position.

Damped harmonic motion

$$\frac{d^2x}{dt^2} + \alpha\frac{dx}{dt} + \omega^2x = 0 \quad \text{for } \alpha > 0$$

The roots of the auxiliary equation are λ_1 and λ_2.

Overdamping (heavy damping) $\alpha > 2\omega$, $x = Ae^{\lambda_1 t} + Be^{\lambda_2 t}$

Critical damping $\alpha = 2\omega$, $x = (A + Bt)e^{\left(-\frac{\alpha}{2}t\right)}$

Underdamping (light damping) $\alpha < 2\omega$, $x = ae^{\left(-\frac{\alpha}{2}t\right)}\sin(pt + \varepsilon)$

where $p = \frac{1}{2}\sqrt{4\omega^2 - \alpha^2}$

Forced oscillations

Undamped $\dfrac{d^2x}{dt^2} + \omega^2x = \omega^2 f(t)$

For $\dfrac{d^2x}{dt^2} + \omega^2x = a\omega^2\sin\Omega t$, **resonance** occurs when $\Omega = \omega$. As $\Omega \to \omega$, the amplitude of the oscillations increases without limit.

Damped $\dfrac{d^2x}{dt^2} + \alpha\dfrac{dx}{dt} + \omega^2x = a\omega^2\sin\Omega t$

Units and dimensions

The three basic dimensions in mechanics are mass, length and time. Other quantities can be expressed in terms of these.

Decision mathematics: Algorithms

Algorithms

An algorithm is a finite set of instructions to solve a problem. For example, the method of multiplying two 3-digit numbers with pen and paper is an algorithm. An algorithm must have

- clearly defined steps,
- generality (it must work for any input),
- a stopping condition (since many algorithms are iterative processes).

Heuristic algorithm One which provides a valid solution but does not necessarily guarantee an optimal solution to the problem.

Greedy algorithm One which gives high immediate rewards without considering possible future consequences. A greedy algorithm does not always give an optimal solution.

Complexity The complexity, or order of an algorithm, is the number of operations needed, in the worst case, expressed as a function of the size of the problem. For example, for a quadratic algorithm, doubling the size of the problem can quadruple the solution size.

Pseudo code A way of writing a computer program that does not rely on the use of a programming language. It can be understood without special training.

Maximin and Minimax

Maximin A problem where you wish to maximise the smallest value of something. For example, you might wish to plan a journey so that the lowest bridge to drive under was as high as possible.

Minimax A problem where you wish to minimise the largest value of something. For example, you might wish to plan a journey so that the longest gap between service stations was as short as possible.

Searching

Linear Every data item is checked.

Binary For ordered data. Repeatedly examines the middle to decide which half contains the target.

Index Search the index to find the page, then search the page.

Packing

First fit Put the next item in the first available slot.

First fit decreasing Order the items in decreasing size. Place the next item in the first available slot.

Full bin Look for combinations of items that will completely fill containers. For leftover items, put each into the first available slot that will take it.

Sorting

Exchange Find the smallest and swap it with the first. Find the next smallest and swap it with the second; etc.

Bubble On the first pass, compare the first with the second and swap if necessary; then compare the second with the third, etc. On the second pass, repeat with all but the last item; etc.

Shuttle Compare and swap, if necessary, items 1 and 2. Then 2 and 3 followed by 1 and 2. Then 3 and 4, followed by 2 and 3, 1 and 2, etc.

Shell Compare and swap items that are not next to each other in the list; this lets an element take bigger steps toward its final position. The list is divided into sublists, each of which is then sorted. Multiple passes over the data are taken with smaller and smaller gap sizes. By the last pass, the array of data will be almost sorted.

Quick

1 Write the data in an array with n columns, where n can be any number less than half the number of pieces of data, giving a number of sublists. The standard value of n is the integer part of $\frac{L}{2}$ where L is the length of the original list.

2 Sort each sublist.

3 Repeat from step 1 using a smaller value of n.

4 When $n = 1$, complete one more sort and stop.

Split the list into two sublists: one with numbers less than or equal to the first number, the other with numbers greater than the first number. Put the first number between the two sublists. Repeat.

Insertion Take a number from the original list and insert it at the correct place in a new list. Repeat.

Decision mathematics: Graphs

Graphs

A graph consists of a number of **vertices** (nodes) connected by edges (arcs).

The order (or degree) of a vertex is the number of edges incident on it.

An **odd vertex** is a vertex with odd degree.

An **even vertex** is a vertex with even degree.

A **digraph** has at least one edge which has a direction associated with it.

A **simple graph** is one with no more than one edge connecting any pair of vertices and which has no loops.

Two vertices in a graph are **connected** if there is an edge joining them. A graph is connected if there is a path between any two vertices.

A **walk** is a continuous journey around a graph. Vertices and edges can be visited more than once.

A **trail** is a walk with no repeated edges.

A **path** is a trail which does not visit any vertex more than once.

A **cycle** is a closed path which starts and ends at the same vertex.

A **Hamilton cycle** (or **Hamiltonian circuit**) is a cycle that visits every vertex once.

An **Euler cycle** is one which travels along every edge exactly once.

An **Eulerian** (or **traversable**) **graph** is one which contains Euler cycles. A graph is Eulerian if and only if all vertices are even.

A **Semi-Eulerian graph** has exactly two odd vertices.

A **planar graph** can be drawn in a plane with no edges crossing.

A **tree** is a simple connected graph with no cycles.

A **spanning tree** is a tree that includes all the vertices in a graph. A **minimum spanning tree** (or **minimum connector**) is a spanning tree of minimum total length.

A **complete graph** has each vertex joined to every other vertex. K_5 is the complete graph with five vertices.

A **bipartite graph** has two sets of vertices, often a right-hand set of vertices and a left-hand set of vertices. Each edge joins a vertex in one set with a vertex in the other set.

The **adjacency** (or **incidence**) **matrix** for a graph has its rows and columns labelled with the vertices of the graph and the entries show the number of edges from vertex i to vertex j.

A **network** is a graph in which the edges have weights associated with them.

The entries in a **distance matrix** show the weights between vertices in a network.

The **route matrix** shows the next vertex on the route from the start vertex to the destination vertex.

Dynamic programming

Dynamic programming is a technique which can be used to solve some optimisation problems modelled by networks, though the solution is usually presented in a tabular form. In a dynamic programming network, the nodes are referred to as **states**, directed arcs are called **actions** and the transition from one state to the next is a **stage**. The optimal plan in a dynamic programming problem consists of maximising or minimising the **value** of a sequence of actions taking you through all the stages.

Working backwards from the endpoint, at each stage find the best strategy from there to the end. This is a **sub-optimal strategy**. Go back another stage and repeat until you get back to the beginning.

Decision mathematics: Networks

Minimum connector

Prim's algorithm
Start at an arbitrary vertex. At each stage connect in the vertex which is nearest to the current connected set.

Kruskal's algorithm
At each stage select the shortest unselected edge, provided that in doing so a cycle is not formed.

Shortest path

Dijkstra's algorithm
At each stage label a vertex and then update the working values on the vertices connected to the newly labelled vertex by replacing the old working value by label + distance (if less). Trace back to find the route when the destination vertex is labelled.

Floyd's algorithm
Finds all the shortest paths in a network by updating the distance and route matrices. The update of the distance matrix uses the triple operation to see, in turn, if it is better to go via intermediate vertices. If at the kth iteration the distance from vertex i to vertex j is reduced, then the new (i, j) entry in the route matrix is the (i, k) entry in the previous route matrix, i.e. the corresponding entry from column k (see below).

Triple operation
For each iteration, there is a chosen row and column in the distance matrix. Other elements in the distance matrix are compared with the sum of corresponding entries in the chosen row and column. They are replaced with the sum if it is smaller.

Distance matrix at the end of iteration 2

	A	B	C	D
A	14	7	2	11
B	7	14	3	4
C	2	3	4	2
D	11	4	7	15

Iteration 3 for distance matrix

	A	B	C	D
A	4	5	2	4
B	5	6	3	4
C	2	3	4	2
D	9	4	7	9

Route matrix at the end of iteration 2

	A	B	C	D
A	B	B	C	B
B	A	A	C	D
C	A	B	A	D
D	B	B	B	B

Iteration 3 for route matrix

	A	B	C	D
A	C	C	C	C
B	C	C	C	D
C	A	B	A	D
D	B	B	B	B

New entries in the route matrix are those in the corresponding row of the highlighted column **if** the distance has changed.

Route inspection (Chinese postman, or postperson)

The problem of finding the least-weight cycle which travels along every edge in a network: an Euler cycle, if one exists. If the network is not Eulerian, consider all possible pairings of odd vertices. For each pairing find the minimum cost of connecting the vertices in their pairs. Choose the pairing with the least cost and use the associated edges twice.

Travelling salesman (or salesperson)

In the classical problem the aim is to visit each vertex only once by using a complete network of shortest distances. Revisiting vertices is allowed in the practical problem. Start by converting a practical problem to a classical problem by finding the shortest connection between each pair of vertices.

Nearest neighbour algorithm
Start at an arbitrary vertex, go to the nearest unvisited vertex. Continue till all the vertices have been visited then return to the starting vertex.

Upper bound
Use the nearest neighbour algorithm to find a Hamilton cycle. Any Hamilton cycle is an upper bound.

Lower bound
Delete a vertex and the edges incident on it. Find the minimum connector of the remainder of the network. Reconnect the deleted vertex using the two smallest removed edges.

To obtain upper and lower bounds for a travelling salesman problem:

- starting the nearest neighbour at each vertex in turn, the best upper bound is the least upper bound as this is nearest the optimal solution (minimax).
- deleting each vertex in turn, the best lower bound is the greatest lower bound (maximin).

Interpret the classical solution in terms of the original practical problem. (Revisiting vertices is allowed in the practical problem.) Find a tour which satisfies the bounds established. Tour improvement can be achieved by modifying the existing tour heuristically.

Decision mathematics: Critical path analysis and network flows

Critical path analysis

An activity is a task which takes time and/or resources to complete.

Precedence tables show the activities that need to be done, together with their duration and their immediate precedents.

Precedence networks show the sequence of the activities. There are two types of networks:

Activity on arc networks have one start event and one end event.

Activity on node networks have one start activity and one end activity.

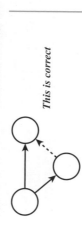

e_i	l_i

e_j	l_j

Activity duration d

Activity duration d	
Earliest start	Earliest finish

Activity duration d	
Earliest start	Earliest finish

e_i = early time for event i
l_i = late time for event i

An event is the start or finish of one or more activities.

Dummy activities are used in activity on arc networks to keep the correct logic and to ensure each activity is uniquely defined by (i, j) where i is the starting event and j is the finishing event, as shown in the diagrams below.

This is correct

This is incorrect

For activity on arc networks

Forward pass	early time = $\max(e_i + d)$ for all activities arriving at node j
Backward pass	late time = $\min(l_j - d)$ for all activities leaving node i
Critical activity	One for which $l_j - e_i = d$
Total float	$l_j - e_i - d$
Independent float	$e_j - l_i - d$

Cascade charts and resources

Cascade chart	This shows the order of activities in a project against a time scale. Also known as a Gantt chart.
Resource histogram	This shows the quantity of resources (usually the number of people) needed to do the activities at any given time in a project.
Resource levelling	When planning a project, it may be desirable to minimise the resources at any given time or to complete the project as quickly or as cheaply as possible. Altering the resource histogram to achieve this is called resource levelling.

Network flows

Begin with an initial feasible flow. Improve the flow by finding flow-augmenting paths, increasing the flow along them as much as possible, and then relabelling potential flows and backflows in each of its arcs.

For a directed arc, potential backflow = flow.

For a non-directed arc, potential backflow = capacity + flow.

A cut splits the vertices into two sets: one including the source and one including the sink. The capacity of a cut is the total of all the cut arcs with direction going from source to sink. If the network has minimum capacities, the capacity of the cut is the sum of the upper capacities in the cut edges with direction going from source to sink minus the sum of the lower capacities in the cut edges with direction going from sink to source.

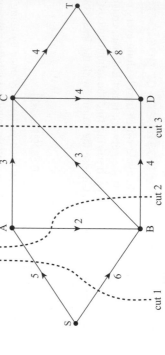

Maximum flow–minimum cut theorem

The capacity of the minimum cut = the maximum flow

If a network has more than one source, introduce a single super-source feeding into all of them; similarly for more than one sink.

Matchings

A matching maps vertices in one set to vertices in a second set. No vertex may be used more than once.

Improve a matching by finding an alternating path of edges which are alternately not in and in the current matching, finishing with one that is not in the current matching. The solution consists of edges *in* the alternating path but *not in* the initial matching and edges *in* the initial matching but *not in* the alternating path.

A matching is maximal if no more edges can be added to it.

A complete matching pairs every vertex in set X to one in set Y and is only possible if X and Y have the same number of vertices.

Allocation problems

When a matching problem also involves costs, then a method is needed for finding a minimum-cost solution. Such problems can be solved using linear programming.

The Hungarian algorithm

This algorithm works by increasing the number of zeros in the matrix. For minimisation of costs, follow these steps.

1 If the cost matrix is not square, add in dummy row(s) or column(s) of equal numbers to make it square.

2 Subtract the minimum entry in each row from all the entries in the row.

3 Repeat step 2 for the columns.

4 Draw the minimum number of horizontal and/or vertical lines to cover all the zeros.

5 If the number of lines is equal to the number of columns in the matrix, the positions of the zeros indicate an optimal matching; if not, go to step 6.

6 Find the smallest element not covered; subtract it from the non-covered elements and add it to any elements covered by two lines.

7 Go to step 2.

For maximisation of profits, subtract the values in each row/column from the maximum numbers in the row/column.

Transportation problems

An extension of the allocation problem occurs when there is a number of allocations to make with constraints on the supply and demand. Such problems can be solved using linear programming.

In a balanced transportation problem, the total demand = the total supply.

An initial feasible solution must be obtained. One method for doing this is the north–west corner method: supply as much from the first source to the first destination as you can, then use up any remaining supply for the second destination. If all the demand has not been satisfied, get as much as you can from the second source and repeat until all the supply is used up and all the demand satisfied.

Finding an optimal solution in a transportation problem involves evaluating each unused cell to determine whether a shift into it is advantageous from a total-cost standpoint. If it is, the shift is made and the process is repeated. When all the cells have been evaluated and appropriate shifts made, the problem is solved. One approach to making this evaluation is the stepping stone method.

Simulation (Monte Carlo methods)

Realisations of a uniform random variable (e.g. generated by a die or using random number tables) are transformed to give realisations of occurrences in the real world.

Simulation of situations involving queuing

The queuing discipline is the rule determining the order in which customers are served.

The inter-arrival time is the time between the arrival of one customer into the system and the arrival of the next.

The service time is the time taken to serve a customer, i.e. after queuing.

Verification and validation

Verification   Checking that a model works in accordance with its specifications.

Validation   Checking that a model reflects reality.

Decision mathematics: Linear programming

Technical terms

The **objective function** is a linear function of the decision variables, which is to be optimised.

Constraints are bounds on the values which the decision variables can take on their own or in combination.

The **feasible region** is the set of all points which satisfy all of the constraints.

The **optimal solution** occurs at one vertex (or, exceptionally, along one edge) of the feasible region.

In **graphical linear programming**, problems in two (or three) dimensions can be solved by identifying the vertices of the feasible region from a graph.

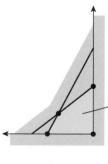

feasible region

The simplex algorithm

Slack variables are used to convert an inequality into an equality.
For example, $2x + 3y \leqslant 12$ converts to $2x + 3y + s = 12$.

The standard linear programming problem is to **maximise**, subject to $\leqslant$ constraints.

1 Convert the inequalities to equalities using slack variables.

2 Represent the problem in a tableau.

3 Use the objective row to find the pivot column.

4 Use the ratio test to find the pivot element.

5 Divide through the pivot row by the pivot element.

6 Add or subtract multiples of the transformed pivot row to or from the other rows to create zeros in the pivot column.

7 Repeat until there are no negatives in the objective row (or positives if minimising).

8 Set basic variables (with columns containing a single 1 with the rest of the entries 0) to corresponding values in the RHS and set non-basic variables to zero.

Problems involving $\geqslant$ constraints

There are two methods for dealing with problems with $\geqslant$ constraints with the simplex method: two-stage simplex and the big M method.

Two-stage simplex

1 Introduce artificial variables to $=$ and $\geqslant$ constraints.

2 Define a supplementary objective function: the sum of the artificial variables.

3 Express the supplementary objective in terms of the other variables by eliminating the artificial variables.

4 Use simplex to minimise the supplementary objective, keeping track of the original objective.

5 If the minimum value of the supplementary objective is greater than zero, conclude that there is no feasible solution to the original problem.

6 If the minimum value of the supplementary objective is zero, then you have a feasible solution to the original problem. Discard the supplementary objective and the artificial variables and use simplex to proceed to the optimal solution.

Big M method

1 Introduce artificial variables to $=$ and $\geqslant$ constraints.

2 Define the objective function as in the ordinary form of the simplex algorithm then subtract some arbitrarily large number, M, multiplied by the sum of the artificial variables. For example, $P = 3x + 2y + 7z - M(a_1 + a_2)$.

3 Express the objective function in terms of the other variables by eliminating the artificial variables.

4 Use the simplex algorithm until there are no more negative entries in the objective row.

5 Set basic variables (with columns containing a single 1 with the rest of the entries 0) to corresponding values in the RHS and set non-basic variables to zero.

Decision mathematics: Decision analysis and game theory

Decision analysis

When analysing a decision-making process, a decision tree can be constructed. A decision tree has three kinds of nodes; the EMV (see below) is worked out at chance nodes and the best course of action is selected at decision nodes.

Decision node

Chance node

Payoff node

EMV   Expected monetary value (the average gain in the long run).

Utility function   A function which allows for £1 gain (for example) being more important to some people than to others.

Game theory

In a two-person, zero-sum game, one person's gain is the same as the other's loss.

A payoff matrix represents the gain for a player for each combination of strategies for the two players in a two-person game.

Finding a play-safe strategy for a zero-sum game

In the payoff matrix for A:

1 find the lowest term in each row. A will use the strategy that involves the highest of these values (i.e. maximin).

2 find the highest term in each column. B will use the strategy that involves the lowest of these values (i.e. minimax).

Stable solution

The play-safe solution is a stable solution if A assumes B uses his play-safe strategy but can do no better by using an alternative strategy and B assumes A uses his play-safe strategy but can do no better by using an alternative strategy. In this case,

the highest(lowest term in each row) = the lowest(highest term in each column).

A stable solution is sometimes called a saddle point.

Dominance

Looking at the payoff matrix for player A, if all the elements of one row are smaller than the corresponding elements of another row then A would never use that strategy. You can eliminate it and say that it is dominated by the more favourable strategy.

Finding a mixed strategy using a graph

1 If player A has two possible strategies, assume he adopts the first strategy with probability p and the second with probability $1 - p$.

2 The expected payoff for A will depend on the choices B makes.

3 Plot A's expected payoffs on a graph.

4 Analyse the results. In the example shown below, B will not play strategy 1 as it will maximise A's gain. A's best strategy is to play with the value of p given by the intersection of the other two lines. This maximises A's minimum return (i.e. maximin).

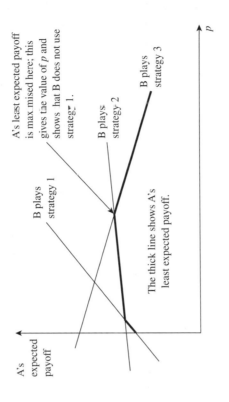

A's expected payoff

B plays strategy 1

B plays strategy 2

B plays strategy 3

A's least expected payoff is max mixed here; this gives the value of p and shows that B does not use strategy 1.

The thick line shows A's least expected payoff.

p

Finding a mixed strategy using the simplex algorithm

1 If player A has more than two strategies, call the probabilities of each p_1, p_2, p_3, etc.

2 If there are any negative elements in the payoff matrix, add k to make them all positive.

3 This is one way to formulate the linear programming problem.

Maximise $V - k$ (this is A's expected payoff from the original game).
(V is the expected payoff from the game which has all positive elements in the payoff matrix.)

Subject to $V \leqslant$ expected payoff if B plays strategy 1
$V \leqslant$ expected payoff if B plays strategy 2 etc.

$$p_1 + p_2 + p_3 + \ldots \leqslant 1$$

and

$$p_1, p_2, p_3, \ldots \geqslant 0$$

Decision mathematics: Logic and recurrence relations

Logic

Propositional calculus

p and q are propositions (statements) that can be true or false. Compound propositions are made using propositional connectives, or logical operators (see below).

Boolean algebra

A system of symbolic logic similar in form to algebra but dealing with logical rather than numerical relationships, and the operations 'and', 'or', and 'not'.

Propositional connectives

$\vee$	or	$\wedge$	and	$\sim$	not
$\Longleftrightarrow$	equivalence	$\Rightarrow$	implies		

If a statement is false then it is often given the number 0, but if it is true then it is given the number 1. These are called **Boolean variables** and they can take only two values. This can be used to construct **truth tables**.

Identity laws

$p \wedge 1 = p$ $p \vee 1 = 1$
$p \vee 0 = p$ $p \wedge 0 = 0$

Associative laws

$(p \vee q) \vee r = p \vee (q \vee r)$
$(p \wedge q) \wedge r = p \wedge (q \wedge r)$

Commutative laws

$p \vee q = q \vee p$
$p \wedge q = q \wedge p$

Distributive laws

$p \wedge (q \vee r) = (p \wedge q) \vee (p \wedge r)$
$p \vee (q \wedge r) = (p \vee q) \wedge (p \vee r)$

De Morgan's laws

$\sim (p \wedge q) \Longleftrightarrow (\sim p) \vee (\sim q)$
$\sim (p \vee q) \Longleftrightarrow (\sim p) \wedge (\sim q)$

Double negation

$\sim (\sim p) = p$

Complement laws

$p \vee \sim p = 1$
$p \wedge \sim p = 0$

Absorption laws

$p \wedge p = p$ $p \wedge (p \vee q) = p$
$p \vee p = p$ $p \vee (p \wedge q) = p$

Truth table

p	q	$p \wedge q$
1	1	1
1	0	0
0	1	0
0	0	0

Boolean algebra is one of the main ideas in the development of electronics. **Logic gates** are used in the representation of electronic circuits.

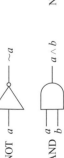

NOT a — $\sim a$

AND $\begin{array}{c} a \\ b \end{array}$ — $a \wedge b$

OR $\begin{array}{c} a \\ b \end{array}$ — $a \vee b$

NAND $\begin{array}{c} a \\ b \end{array}$ — $\sim (a \wedge b)$

Recurrence relations

First order

For $u_{n+1} = au_n + f(n)$ $(a \neq 1)$

Homogeneous

$f(n) = 0$, $u_n = a^n u_0$

Non-homogeneous

$f(n) \neq 0$, $u_n = Aa^n + \text{particular solution}$

For $u_{n+1} = u_n + f(n)$ (i.e. $a = 1$ in the relation above),

$$u_{n+1} = u_0 + \sum_{i=0}^{n} f(i)$$

Second order

For $u_{n+2} + au_{n+1} + bu_n = f(n)$
the auxiliary equation is $\lambda^2 + a\lambda + b = 0$ with roots λ_1 and λ_2.

Homogeneous

$f(n) = 0$, $u_n = A\lambda_1^n + B\lambda_2^n$ $(\lambda_1 \neq \lambda_2)$
$u_n = (An + B)\lambda^n$ $(\lambda_1 = \lambda_2 = \lambda)$

Non-homogeneous

$f(n) \neq 0$, a particular solution is added to the corresponding expression for u_n where $f(n) = 0$.

Particular solutions for linear non-homogeneous recurrence relations

$f(n)$	Trial function for particular solution
constant	p
n	$pn + q$
n^2	$pn^2 + qn + r$
k^n	pk^n (or, possibly, pnk^n)

Statistics: Probability

Types of events
A, C

Event
An event is something which may or may not happen; it could be a combination of several outcomes or a single outcome. For example, 'an even number' is an event when rolling a die.

Outcome
An outcome is the result of an experiment or other situation which involves uncertainty; it is one item in the sample space. For example '4' is an outcome when rolling a die.

Exhaustive
A set of exhaustive events covers all possibilities.

Mutually exclusive
Two mutually exclusive events cannot both happen together. For example, 'head' and 'tail' on one toss of one coin are mutually exclusive. For more than two mutually exclusive events, any pair of them are mutually exclusive.

Independent
Independent events can both happen together but don't affect the probability of each other happening. For example, 'head' on one toss of a coin and 'tail' on the next toss of the same coin are independent.

Probability
A, C

For a discrete distribution in which all outcomes are equally likely,

$$\text{Probability} = \frac{\text{The number of required outcomes}}{\text{The total number of possible outcomes}}$$

For a continuous distribution, the probability is the relevant area under the graph of the probability density function.

Notation

A and B are events. A' is the event 'not A'.
$A \cap B$ is 'A and B'. $A \cup B$ is 'A or B or both'.
$A \mid B$ is 'A given B'.

Probability of an event not happening
$P(A') = 1 - P(A)$

Probability of two events
$P(A \cup B) = P(A) + P(B) - P(A \cap B)$
For mutually exclusive events, $P(A \cup B) = P(A) + P(B)$

Conditional probability
C, E

$$P(A \text{ given } B) = P(A \mid B) = \frac{P(A \cap B)}{P(B)}$$

$$P(A \text{ and } B) = P(A \cap B) = P(A) \times P(B \mid A) = P(B) \times P(A \mid B)$$

For independent events

$P(B \mid A) = P(B) \Leftrightarrow B$ and A are independent.
If B and A are independent, $P(A \cap B) = P(A) \times P(B)$

Bayes' theorem
If $A_1, A_2, \ldots, A_n$ is a set of mutually exclusive and exhaustive events and B is any event then $P(A_j \mid B) = \dfrac{P(A_j) \times P(B \mid A_j)}{P(B)}$

where $P(B) = \sum\limits_{i=1}^{n} P(A_i) \times P(B \mid A_i)$ and $1 \le j \le n$.

Arrangements and selections
C

Arrangements
Number of ways of arranging n unlike objects in line
$$n!$$

Combinations
Number of ways of selecting r objects from n unlike objects (order does not matter)
$$^nC_r = \binom{n}{r} = \frac{n!}{r!(n-r)!}$$

Permutations
Number of ways of selecting r objects from n unlike objects (order matters)
$$^nP_r = \frac{n!}{(n-r)!}$$

$$^nC_r = \frac{^nP_r}{r!}$$

Statistics: Analysing data

Types of data

Bimodal distribution	A distribution with two modes. If they are not adjacent values, then one could have a higher frequency than the other. The diagram on the right shows the shape of a histogram which a bimodal distribution represents.
Unimodal distribution	A distribution with only one mode.
Bivariate data	Data in which two variables are recorded for each data item. The values can be represented as pairs of co-ordinates on a scatter diagram.
Categorical data	The data are in categories; they are not numerical. Sometimes known as qualitative data.
Continuous data	Continuous data are measured on a scale; they can be represented by a section of the number line. For any two possible values, you could always find another possible value between them.
Discrete data	Discrete data may only take certain separate values, for example whole numbers or values in steps of a quarter. There are either a finite number of possible values or an infinite number of possible values which could be written in an ordered list without missing any out.
Quantitative data	Numerical data; this term is used to describe both continuous and discrete data.
Interval scale	The zero on an interval scale is set at an arbitrary value so the differences between measurements are meaningful but ratios between measurements are not. For example, it is meaningful to say that one temperature is 10 degrees more than another but not that it is twice as much.
Ratio scale	This has a true zero, in contrast with an interval scale. For example, height: a plant 20 cm high is twice the height of one 10 cm high.

Extrapolation and interpolation

When extrapolating from data, you estimate results that go beyond the range of the data you have. The further you go from the data, the less reliance can be placed on the results.

When interpolating, you are estimating results within the range of the data you have.

Measures of central tendency (averages)

Average	A single value that is representative of all the data. In everyday speech this is usually the mean, but the mode, median and mid-range are also types of average.
Arithmetic mean	Often referred to as 'the average' in everyday speech. For a set of n data items, $x_1, x_2, \ldots, x_n$, the arithmetic mean is given by $\bar{x} = \dfrac{x_1 + x_2 + \ldots + x_n}{n}$. For a sample of n observations of x, there being f_i readings of x_i (i.e. f_i is the frequency of x_i), $\bar{x} = \dfrac{\sum x_i f_i}{n}$ where $\sum f_i = n$.
Geometric mean	The geometric mean is $\sqrt[n]{x_1 x_2 x_3 \ldots x_n}$
Harmonic mean	$\dfrac{1}{\text{harmonic mean}} = \dfrac{1}{x_1} + \dfrac{1}{x_2} + \ldots + \dfrac{1}{x_n}$
Median	The value of the middle item when data are put in order. For an even number of data items, it is the mean of the values of the middle two.
Mid-range	A value half-way between the largest and smallest values in a data set.
Mode	The most frequently occurring value in a data set.

Measures of dispersion

Interquartile range	$IQR = $ upper quartile $-$ lower quartile
Mean square deviation (This is sometimes called variance.)	$msd = \dfrac{S_{xx}}{n}$
Root mean square deviation (This is sometimes called standard deviation.)	$rmsd = \sqrt{msd}$
Variance (or sample variance)	$s^2 = \dfrac{S_{xx}}{n-1}$
Standard deviation (or sample standard deviation)	$s = \sqrt{s^2}$
Sum of squares of deviations	$S_{xx} = \sum (x_i - \bar{x})^2 f_i = \sum x_i^2 f_i - \dfrac{\left(\sum x_i f_i\right)^2}{n} = \sum x_i^2 f_i - n\bar{x}^2$

Coding

If $y = a + bx$ then $\bar{y} = a + b\bar{x}$, $s_y^2 = b^2 s_x^2$

Statistics: Analysing data

Ranking

When data are put in order, the **quartiles** divide the distribution into four equally-sized groups. The median is the second quartile.

Percentiles divide ranked data into 100 equally-sized groups.

Box-and-whisker plots

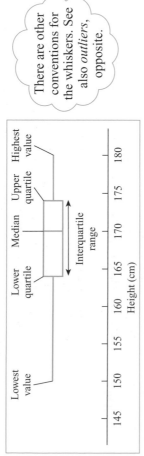

At least two box-and-whisker plots are usually drawn, on the same scale, to compare related sets of data.

There are other conventions for the whiskers. See also outliers, opposite.

Histograms

A, C

The **area** of each bar is proportional to the frequency.

Frequency density can be calculated by dividing the frequency for a class by its width.

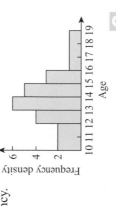

Skew (skewness)

C

A skewed distribution of data is not symmetrical. The diagrams on the right show the shapes of histograms and box-and-whisker plots for skewed data. Usually there are the following relationships between median and mean for skewed data.

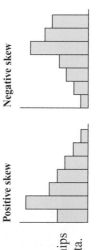

Positive skew
median < mean

Negative skew
median > mean

Contingency table

A, C

A two-way table showing one characteristic on the rows and one in the columns. For continuous data, the data will be grouped.

	Male	Female
Right-handed	32	28
Left-handed	7	5

Outliers

C

An outlier is an unusual data item. It may be a mistake or an indication that there is something wrong or it may be a genuine data item that is unusual.

Outliers using the interquartile range

A data item may be regarded as an outlier if it is more than 1.5 times the interquartile range above the upper quartile **or** below the lower quartile. On a box-and-whisker plot, this is sometimes shown as a cross, with the whisker stopping at the next highest (or lowest) data item.

Outliers using the standard deviation

An item of data may be regarded as an outlier if it is more than two standard deviations away from the mean.

Notation

C

Greek letters are often used for parameters and Roman ones for sample statistics.

Parameter A quantity used in defining the distribution of a population; for example μ or σ

μ The population mean
σ The population standard deviation

Statistic A value calculated from the data; for example $\bar{x}$ or s

$\bar{x}$ The sample mean
s The sample standard deviation

A caret ('hat') is often used in a general way to indicate an estimate of a population parameter; for example

$\hat{\mu}$ An estimate of the population mean
$\hat{\sigma}$ An estimate of the population standard deviation

Caution
The notations s, σ and $\hat{\sigma}$ are sometimes used differently for the square root of the sample variance by different calculator manufacturers, authors and users.

Statistics: Sampling, correlation and regression

Sums of squares and products

For a sample of n pairs of observations (x_i, y_i)

$$S_{xx} = \sum (x_i - \bar{x})^2 = \sum x_i^2 - \frac{(\sum x_i)^2}{n} = \sum x_i^2 - n\bar{x}^2$$

$$S_{yy} = \sum (y_i - \bar{y})^2 = \sum y_i^2 - \frac{(\sum y_i)^2}{n} = \sum y_i^2 - n\bar{y}^2$$

$$S_{xy} = \sum (x_i - \bar{x})(y_i - \bar{y}) = \sum x_i y_i - \frac{(\sum x_i)(\sum y_i)}{n} = \sum x_i y_i - n(\bar{x})(\bar{y})$$

Correlation and regression

Product moment correlation coefficient: Pearson's coefficient

$$r = \frac{S_{xy}}{\sqrt{S_{xx}S_{yy}}} = \frac{\sum (x_i - \bar{x})(y_i - \bar{y})}{\sqrt{\sum (x_i - \bar{x})^2 \times \sum (y_i - \bar{y})^2}}$$

Rank correlation: Spearman's coefficient

Spearman's coefficient is Pearson's coefficient for rankings.

$$r_s = 1 - \frac{6\sum d_i^2}{n(n^2 - 1)}$$

where $d_i = x_i - y_i$, and x_i and y_i denote ranks of data

Regression

Least squares regression line of y on x

$$y - \bar{y} = b(x - \bar{x}) \quad \text{where } b = \frac{S_{xy}}{S_{xx}} = \frac{\sum (x_i - \bar{x})(y_i - \bar{y})}{\sum (x_i - \bar{x})^2}$$

For bivariate data, you are often interested in whether one variable affects the other. The one affected is the dependent (response) variable; the one causing the effect is the independent (explanatory) variable.

Residuals

The residual is the difference between the measured value of the dependent variable and that calculated from the model, i.e. it is $y - \hat{y}$ where y is the measured value and $\hat{y}$ is the estimate from the model. In simple linear regression, the least squares regression line minimises the sum of the squares of the residuals. More generally, the method of least squares for fitting a model minimises the sum of the squares of the residuals.

Sampling

Population — The population is all the items under consideration. The word is also used for the complete set of values of a variable.

Sample — A sample is a set of items chosen from a population.

Sampling frame — A sampling frame is a list of the population; it enables a sample to be chosen.

Sampling unit — A sampling unit is a member of a sample.

Census — In a census, every member of the population is included.

Survey — An investigation of the characteristics of a population. This often involves sampling and the use of a questionnaire.

Cluster sample — In cluster sampling, the population is divided into groups or clusters, each of which is thought to behave in broadly the same way as the entire population. Some clusters (often only one or two) are selected at random and a sample (or a complete census) is taken of each selected cluster.

Opportunity sample — A sample which may be obtained conveniently.

Quota sample — In a quota sample, the number of items to sample from each subgroup is specified in advance. This is often used in market research interviews where the choice of people to ask is left to the interviewer as long as s/he fulfils the quota set.

Random sample — Each individual is chosen entirely by chance and each member of the population has a known, but not necessarily equal, chance of being included in the sample.

Simple random sample — Every possible sample has an equal probability of being chosen.

Stratified sample — In stratified sampling, the population is divided into subgroups, or strata, which are anticipated to behave differently. (A common example is males and females.) A sample is taken from each, usually using simple random sampling. If the size of the sample from each subgroup is proportional to the size of the subgroup from which it is taken, this is proportional stratified sampling.

Systematic sample — In systematic sampling, items are chosen at regular intervals from the sampling frame, for example, every 30th item.

Statistics: Distributions

Discrete distributions

X is a random variable taking values x_i in a discrete distribution with **probability distribution** $P(X = x_i) = p_i$, where $\sum p_i = 1$

Expectation $\quad \mu = E(X) = \sum x_i p_i$

Variance $\quad \sigma^2 = \mathrm{Var}(X) = E[(X - \mu)^2] = E(X^2) - \mu^2$
$$= \sum (x_i - \mu)^2 p_i = \sum x_i^2 p_i - \mu^2$$

Standard deviation σ is the standard deviation. $\sigma = \sqrt{\text{variance}}$

Continuous distributions

X is a continuous random variable with **probability density function** (p.d.f.) $f(x)$

Expectation $\quad \mu = E(X) = \int_{\text{all values}} x f(x)\, dx$

Variance $\quad \sigma^2 = \mathrm{Var}(X) = E[(X - \mu)^2] = E(X^2) - \mu^2$
$$= \int (x - \mu)^2 f(x)\, dx = \int x^2 f(x)\, dx - \mu^2$$

Standard deviation σ is the standard deviation.

Properties of the p.d.f.

$f(x) \geq 0$ $\qquad\qquad$ $f(x) = F'(x)$

$P(c \leq X \leq d) = \int_c^d f(x)\, dx$ $\qquad$ $\int_{\text{all values}} f(x)\, dx = 1$

The mode of X is where the p.d.f. has its maximum value.
The mean of X is its expected value.
The median of X is the value which has half the area under the p.d.f. curve on each side of it, i.e. $F(m) = \frac{1}{2}$, where m is the median.

Cumulative distribution function (c.d.f.)

$F(x) = P(X \leq x) = \int_{-\infty}^x f(t)\, dt$

Continuity correction

If a continuous distribution is being used as an approximation for a discrete distribution (for example Normal approximation to a binomial or Poisson distribution), it is necessary to use a continuity correction. For example, $P(X > 5)$ for the discrete distribution becomes $P(X \geq 5.5)$ for the continuous one because all the numbers from 5.5 upwards would round to more than 5. Similarly, $P(X \geq 5)$ would become $P(X \geq 4.5)$ and $P(X = 5)$ becomes $P(4.5 \leq X < 5.5)$.

Bivariate distributions

Covariance

$\mathrm{Cov}(X, Y) = E[(X - E(X))(Y - E(Y))] = E(XY) - E(X)E(Y)$
$\mathrm{Cov}(X, Y) = 0$ if X and Y are independent.
$\mathrm{Var}(aX \pm bY) = a^2\mathrm{Var}(X) + b^2\mathrm{Var}(Y) \pm 2ab\mathrm{Cov}(X, Y)$

Population correlation coefficient $\rho = \dfrac{\mathrm{Cov}(X, Y)}{\sigma_X \sigma_Y}$

Expectation and variance

$\left.\begin{array}{l} E(a + bX) = a + bE(X) \\ \mathrm{Var}(a + bX) = b^2\mathrm{Var}(X) \end{array}\right\}$ for discrete and continuous random variables

Expectation of functions

For a function $g(X)$

$E[g(X)] = \sum g(x_i)p(x_i)$ $\quad$ (discrete random variable)
$E[g(X)] = \int g(x)f(x)\, dx$ $\quad$ (continuous random variable)
$\mathrm{Var}[g(X)] = E[\{g(X) - E[g(X)]\}^2] = E[\{g(X)\}^2] - [E\{g(X)\}]^2$

For random variables X and Y (discrete or continuous)
$E(X + Y) = E(X) + E(Y)$ $\quad$ $E(aX \pm bY) = aE(X) \pm bE(Y)$
If X, Y are independent the following three results hold.
$\mathrm{Var}(X \pm Y) = \mathrm{Var}(X) + \mathrm{Var}(Y)$, $\quad$ $\mathrm{Var}(aX \pm bY) = a^2\mathrm{Var}(X) + b^2\mathrm{Var}(Y)$
and $E(XY) = E(X) \times E(Y)$

The Normal distribution

Standardisation $\quad X \sim N(\mu, \sigma^2) \quad \Rightarrow \quad \dfrac{X - \mu}{\sigma} = Z \sim N(0, 1)$

where $\sim$ denotes 'has the distribution'.

The Central Limit Theorem

For random samples of size n drawn from a distribution with mean μ and finite variance σ^2, the distribution of $\bar{X}$ approaches $N\left(\mu, \dfrac{\sigma^2}{n}\right)$ as n increases.

Linear combinations of random variables

If X has a Normal distribution then so does $aX + b$.
If X and Y have independent Normal distributions then $aX + bY$ has a Normal distribution.
If X and Y have independent Poisson distributions then $X + Y$ has a Poisson distribution.

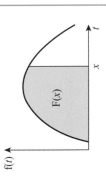

Statistics: Estimation and generating functions

Estimation

E

An estimator is a statistic, calculated from a sample, used to estimate a parameter of the whole population, such as the mean or variance.

Unbiased estimator

An unbiased estimator has an expected value which is equal to the population parameter it is estimating.

Consistent estimator

Consistent estimators become more precise as the sample size gets larger, i.e. 'they get the right answer for large samples'. Formally, a consistent estimator is one for which the probability of differing from the actual value of the parameter by more than an arbitrarily small quantity tends to zero as the sample size increases. One criterion for checking this is that the variance of a consistent estimator approaches zero as the sample size increases. This criterion can only be used if the estimator is unbiased or if any bias itself approaches zero as the sample size increases.

Standard error

The standard error of a sample statistic is a name sometimes given to the standard deviation of its distribution.

Unbiased estimators from a single sample

For a population mean, μ

$$\bar{X} = \frac{1}{n}\sum X_i \qquad \mathrm{Var}(\bar{X}) = \frac{\sigma^2}{n}$$

For population variance, σ^2

$$S^2 = \frac{1}{n-1}\sum(X_i - \bar{X})^2$$

Pooled unbiased estimators from two samples

For a population mean, μ

$$\bar{X} = \frac{n_1\bar{X}_1 + n_2\bar{X}_2}{n_1 + n_2}$$

For a population variance, σ^2

$$S^2 = \frac{(n_1 - 1)S_1^2 + (n_2 - 1)S_2^2}{n_1 + n_2 - 2}$$

Bias

$$\mathrm{Bias}(\hat{\theta}) = \mathrm{E}(\hat{\theta}) - \theta$$

Mean square error, $\mathrm{MSE}(\hat{\theta}) = \mathrm{E}[(\hat{\theta} - \theta)^2] = \mathrm{Var}(\hat{\theta}) + [\mathrm{Bias}(\hat{\theta})]^2$

Efficiency of an estimator

E

One estimator is more **efficient** than another if it has smaller mean square error for all values of the parameter.

For two unbiased estimators, the more efficient one is the one with the smaller variance for all values of the parameter. The **relative efficiency** of T_1 compared with T_2 for two unbiased estimators, T_1 and T_2, is $\dfrac{\mathrm{Var}(T_2)}{\mathrm{Var}(T_1)}$.

Maximum likelihood estimation

The maximum likelihood estimator of θ is given by $\dfrac{\mathrm{dL}(\theta)}{\mathrm{d}\theta} = 0$

where $\mathrm{L}(\theta)$ is the likelihood expressed as a function of the parameter θ.

The likelihood of a set of observations of a continuous random variable

The likelihood is the product of the values of the p.d.f. at each observation.

Confidence intervals

G, E

A 95% confidence interval for a population parameter (e.g. the mean) is an interval calculated from sample data in such a way that, in the long run, in 95% of cases, the interval will include the true value of the parameter. A confidence interval is used as an interval estimate of the parameter.

Generating functions

E

See also page 50.

Probability generating functions (p.g.f.)

For a discrete distribution:

$\mathrm{G}(t) = \mathrm{E}(t^x) = \sum t^x p_x \qquad$ where $p_x = \mathrm{P}(X = x)$

$\mathrm{G}(1) = 1; \quad \mathrm{E}(X) = \mathrm{G}'(1) = \mu; \quad \mathrm{Var}(X) = \mathrm{G}''(1) + \mu - \mu^2$

If $Y = aX + b$ then $\mathrm{G}_Y(t) = t^b \mathrm{G}_X(t^a)$

$\mathrm{G}_{X+Y}(t) = \mathrm{G}_X(t) \times \mathrm{G}_Y(t)$ for independent X and Y

Moment generating functions (m.g.f.)

$\mathrm{M}_X(\theta) = \mathrm{E}(e^{\theta X})$

If $Y = aX + b$ then $\mathrm{M}_Y(\theta) = e^{b\theta}\mathrm{M}_X(a\theta)$

$\mathrm{M}(0) = 1; \quad \mathrm{E}(X) = \mathrm{M}'(0) = \mu; \quad \mathrm{E}(X^n) = \mathrm{M}^{(n)}(0)$
where $\mathrm{M}^{(n)}(\theta)$ denotes differentiation of $\mathrm{M}(\theta)$ n times

$\mathrm{Var}(X) = \mathrm{M}''(0) - [\mathrm{M}'(0)]^2$

$\mathrm{M}_{X+Y}(\theta) = \mathrm{M}_X(\theta) \times \mathrm{M}_Y(\theta)$ for independent X and Y

Statistics: Design and analysis of experiments

Analysis of variance

One-factor model: $x_{ij} = \mu + \alpha_i + \varepsilon_{ij}$ where $\varepsilon_{ij} \sim$ independent $N(0, \sigma^2)$

Source	Sum of squares	Degrees of freedom	Mean square
Between groups	SS_B	$k-1$	$MS_B = \dfrac{SS_B}{k-1}$
Within groups	SS_W	$n-k$	$MS_W = \dfrac{SS_W}{n-k}$
Total	SS_T	$n-1$	

$SS_W = \sum_i \sum_j (x_{ij} - \bar{x}_i)^2$

This is often calculated by subtraction, $SS_W = SS_T - SS_B$.

$$SS_B = \sum_i n_i (\bar{x}_i - \bar{x})^2 = \sum_i \frac{T_i^2}{n_i} - \frac{T^2}{n}$$

$$SS_T = \sum_i \sum_j (x_{ij} - \bar{x})^2 = \sum_i \sum_j x_{ij}^2 - \frac{T^2}{n}$$

Test statistic, $F = \dfrac{MS_B}{MS_W}$

Null distribution $F_{k-1,\, n-k}$

k = number of samples

$\bar{x}_i$ = mean of ith sample

x_{ij} = jth member of ith sample

$\bar{x}$ = overall mean

n_i = size of ith sample

n = total sample size = $\sum_i n_i$

$T_i = \sum_j x_{ij}$

$T = \sum_i \sum_j x_{ij}$

Experimental design

Block   A homogeneous part of the experimental material.

Completely randomised design   The experimental material is assumed to be homogeneous. The treatments are allocated at random to experimental units.

Experiment   A process which results in the collection of data.

Experimental material and treatments   In a statistical experiment, different treatments are applied to experimental material. For example, when different types of seed are trialled in a field, the experimental material is the field and the treatments are the types of seed.

Experimental unit   This is the smallest part of the experimental material which can be given a different treatment. For example, it could be a part of a field. (In this context, the word 'plot' is sometimes used.)

Heterogeneous   Consisting of several different types.

Homogeneous   The same all the way through; uniform.

Latin square   A square containing one of each symbol in each row and each column; an example is shown on the right. This can be used in experimental design. For example, to ensure that three drivers try out three cars over three routes the rows could stand for the drivers, the columns for the routes and A, B, C for the cars.

A	B	C
B	C	A
C	A	B

Paired comparison   Two treatments are applied to the same piece of experimental material or to matched pairs; for example, using different creams on each hand for the same person.

Randomisation   Using random numbers to decide the order in which experiments should be carried out.

Randomised blocks   The experimental material consists of several blocks. The treatments are allocated at random to experimental units within the blocks.

Replication   Repeating an experiment, keeping all conditions the same, as far as possible.

Statistics: Glossary of distributions

Name and type	Function	Mean	Variance	Situations modelled	p.g.f. G(t) (discrete) or m.g.f. M(t)
Binomial $B(n, p)$ *Discrete*	$P(X=r) = {}^nC_r\, p^r q^{n-r}$ for $r = 0, 1, \ldots, n$, $0 < p < 1, q = 1-p$	np	npq	The number of successes in n independent trials of a process in which P(success) = p	$G(t) = (q + pt)^n$
Poisson(λ) *Discrete*	$P(X=r) = e^{-\lambda}\dfrac{\lambda^r}{r!}$ for $r = 0, 1, \ldots$ $\lambda > 0$	λ	λ	The number of occurrences of an event which occurs at a constant average rate independently and at random. It is also used as an approximation to the binomial distribution. $B(n, p) \approx$ Poisson(np) for large n and small p.	$G(t) = e^{\lambda(t-1)}$
Normal $N(\mu, \sigma^2)$ *Continuous*	$f(x) = \dfrac{1}{\sigma\sqrt{2\pi}}\exp\left(-\dfrac{1}{2}\left(\dfrac{x-\mu}{\sigma}\right)^2\right)$ $-\infty < x < \infty$	μ	σ^2	A wide variety of naturally occurring variables. It is also used as an approximation to other distributions (with continuity corrections if discrete). $B(n, p) \approx N(np, npq)$ for $0 \ll p \ll 1$ and large n Poisson$(\lambda) \approx N(\lambda, \lambda)$ for large λ The Central Limit Theorem shows that the sample mean of almost any random variable produces Normality.	$M(\theta) = \exp\left(\mu\theta + \dfrac{1}{2}\sigma^2\theta^2\right)$
Standard Normal $N(0, 1)$ *Continuous*	$f(z) = \dfrac{1}{\sqrt{2\pi}}\exp\left(-\dfrac{1}{2}z^2\right)$ $-\infty < z < \infty$	0	1	As above, with $z = \dfrac{x-\mu}{\sigma}$.	$M(\theta) = \exp\left(\dfrac{1}{2}\theta^2\right)$
Uniform *Discrete*	$P(X=r) = \dfrac{1}{n-m+1}$ $r = m, m+1, \ldots, n$	$\dfrac{m+n}{2}$	$\dfrac{1}{12}(n-m) \times (n-m+2)$	Experiments with equiprobable outcomes (e.g. throwing a fair die).	Not useful
Uniform (Rectangular) on $[a, b]$ *Continuous*	$f(x) = \dfrac{1}{b-a}$ $a \le x \le b$	$\dfrac{a+b}{2}$	$\dfrac{1}{12}(b-a)^2$	Some naturally occurring variables (e.g. used as a model for the error made in rounding a number).	$M(\theta) = \dfrac{e^{b\theta} - e^{a\theta}}{(b-a)\theta}$
Exponential *Continuous*	$f(x) = \lambda e^{-\lambda x}$ $x \ge 0, \lambda > 0$	$\dfrac{1}{\lambda}$	$\dfrac{1}{\lambda^2}$	Some naturally occurring variables (e.g. waiting times).	$M(\theta) = \dfrac{\lambda}{\lambda - \theta}$
Geometric *Discrete*	$P(X=r) = q^{r-1}p$, $r = 1, 2, \ldots$ $0 < p < 1, q = 1-p$	$\dfrac{1}{p}$	$\dfrac{q}{p^2}$	The number of trials needed for the first success in a binomial process.	$G(t) = \dfrac{pt}{1-qt}$
Negative binomial *Discrete*	$P(X=r) = {}^{r-1}C_{n-1}q^{r-n}p^n$ $r = n, n+1, \ldots$ $0 < p < 1, q = 1-p$	$\dfrac{n}{p}$	$\dfrac{nq}{p^2}$	The number of trials needed for n successes in a binomial process; equivalent to n repetitions of the geometric distribution.	$G(t) = \left(\dfrac{pt}{1-qt}\right)^n$

Statistics: Hypothesis testing

Terminology

The data from a sample are used to calculate the value of a **test statistic**.

The test statistic is used to test the **null hypothesis**, H_0, against an **alternative hypothesis**, H_1. The null and alternative hypotheses usually refer to the value of a **parameter** of the **parent population** from which the sample was drawn, with the null hypothesis being that the parameter takes a particular value.

The test statistic is compared with the **critical value** for the test. According to which is more extreme, the null hypothesis is rejected or accepted. The set of values which lead to rejection of H_0 is called the **critical region**. The set of values which lead to acceptance of H_0 is called the **acceptance region**.

For example, for a Normal test with H_0: $\mu = 2.8$ and H_1: $\mu > 2.8$, the critical and acceptance regions are as shown in the diagram.

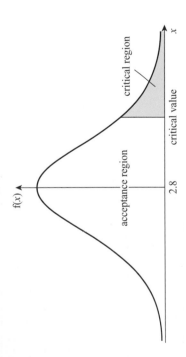

The **critical value** depends on the **significance level** of the test: the probability that, even though H_0 is true, it is incorrectly rejected because of the particular sample chosen.

An alternative hypothesis may be one-sided (e.g. $p > 0.5$), leading to a **1-tail test** as above, or it may be two-sided (e.g. $p \neq 0.5$), leading to a **2-tail test**.

Another way of doing the test is to calculate the probability of an outcome at least as extreme as that observed, on the assumption that the null hypothesis is true. This probability is the level of significance of the data; it is sometimes called the *p*-value. If this probability is less than the significance level of the test, the null hypothesis is rejected; otherwise it is accepted.

By convention, English letters are used for sample statistics and Greek letters for population parameters.

Type I and type II errors

	H_0 accepted	H_0 rejected
H_0 true	Correct result	Type I error
H_0 false	Type II error	Correct result

Power of a test

Power of test $= 1 - \text{P(type II error)}$

Size of a test

The size of a test = significance level = P(type I error)

Operating characteristic

The **operating characteristic** is the probability of a type I error, as a function of the parameter being tested.

For example, for a binomial test with H_0: $p = 0.05$ and H_1: $p > 0.05$, the operating charactistic is as shown in the diagram.

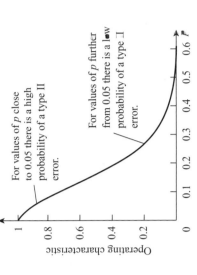

Statistics: Hypothesis tests

Type	Test and distribution	Null hypothesis	Test statistic	Notes
Single sample	Binomial $B(n, p)$	The population value of a probability is some particular value, p.	Observed value, x 'successes' in n trials of a binomial distribution.	See also Normal test on binomial proportion if the sample size is large.
	Poisson(λ)	The population mean has a particular value, λ.	Observed number of occurrences, x, from a Poisson distribution.	
	Normal test for a mean $N(0, 1)$	The population mean has a particular value, μ.	$z = \dfrac{\bar{x} - \mu}{\frac{\sigma}{\sqrt{n}}}$	Exact if $X \sim N(\mu, \sigma^2)$ and σ is known. Approximate if X is not Normal (large sample required). Approximate if σ has to be estimated (large sample required).
	t test for a mean t_{n-1}	The population mean has a particular value, μ.	$t = \dfrac{\bar{x} - \mu}{\frac{s}{\sqrt{n}}}$	The population is Normal, $X \sim N(\mu, \sigma^2)$; s^2 must be calculated with divisor $(n-1)$.
	Wilcoxon signed rank test for a single sample (Wilcoxon single-sample test)	The distribution from which the sample is drawn is symmetrical with population median $= M$.	$T = \min[P, Q]$ P, Q are the sums of the ranks corresponding to positive and negative deviations $(x_i - M)$.	Values of $|x_i - M|$ are ranked; low ranks for small deviations. Normal approximation for large n: Mean $\frac{1}{4}n(n+1)$, Variance $\frac{1}{24}n(n+1)(2n+1)$.
	Normal test on binomial proportion $N(0, 1)$	The population proportion has a given value θ.	$z = \dfrac{p - \theta}{\sqrt{\dfrac{\theta(1-\theta)}{n}}}$ where $p = \dfrac{x}{n}$	The sample size must be large and must not be too close to 0 or 1. The distribution is approximate.
	χ^2 test for variance χ^2_{n-1}	The population variance has a given value σ^2.	$X^2 = \dfrac{(n-1)s^2}{\sigma^2}$	The population is Normal, $X \sim N(\mu, \sigma^2)$; s^2 must be calculated with divisor $(n-1)$.
Other tests	χ^2 test for goodness of fit χ^2_{k-p-1}	The data are drawn from a population with a given distribution.	$X^2 = \sum \dfrac{(f_0 - f_e)^2}{f_e}$	Observations grouped into k cells all with expected frequency ≥ 5; p parameters estimated from data. The distribution is approximate.
	χ^2 test on a contingency table $\chi^2_{(r-1)(c-1)}$	The row and column classifications are independent.	$X^2 = \sum \dfrac{(f_0 - f_e)^2}{f_e}$ If Yates' correction is used, $X^2 = \sum \dfrac{(\lvert f_0 - f_e \rvert - 0.5)^2}{f_e}$	r is the number of rows, c is the number of columns. The distribution is approximate. Expected frequencies ≥ 5. $\left(\text{Expected frequency} = \dfrac{\text{row total} \times \text{column total}}{\text{total sample size}}\right)$ For a χ^2 test on a 2×2 contingency table, some statisticians use Yates' correction.
	Analysis of variance $F_{k-1,\, n-k}$ k samples, $n =$ total size	Samples are drawn from populations with the same mean.	$F = \dfrac{MS_B}{MS_W}$	Samples are drawn from populations with Normal distributions with common variance. See page 49 for more detail.

Statistics: Hypothesis tests

Type	Test and distribution	Null hypothesis	Test statistic	Notes
Correlation (bivariate data)	Pearson's product moment correlation test	The population value of a correlation coefficient, ρ, is zero.	$r = \dfrac{S_{xy}}{\sqrt{S_{xx}S_{yy}}}$	The sample is random and drawn from an (approximately) bivariate Normal distribution. With a large set of data, the scatter diagram for a bivariate Normal distribution is approximately elliptical.
	Spearman's rank correlation test	There is no association between the variables.	$r_s = 1 - \dfrac{6\sum d_i^2}{n(n^2-1)}$	Spearman's test indicates where y is generally increasing (or decreasing) as x increases.
Paired samples	Normal test for paired samples N(0, 1)	The difference in the population means has value k.	$z = \dfrac{(\bar{x}_1 - \bar{x}_2) - k}{\frac{\sigma}{\sqrt{n}}} = \dfrac{\bar{d} - k}{\frac{\sigma}{\sqrt{n}}}$	Treat the differences, d, as a single sample and proceed as in the equivalent single-sample test. This test is not often used.
	t test t_{n-1}	The difference in the population means has value k.	$t = \dfrac{(\bar{x}_1 - \bar{x}_2) - k}{\frac{s}{\sqrt{n}}} = \dfrac{\bar{d} - k}{\frac{s}{\sqrt{n}}}$	Treat the differences, d, as a single sample and proceed as for the single-sample t test. s^2 must be calculated with divisor $(n-1)$ using the differences.
	Wilcoxon signed rank test for paired samples (Wilcoxon paired-sample test)	The median of the differences has value M.	T calculated as for the Wilcoxon single-sample test but using differences	Sample $(x_1, y_1), (x_2, y_2), \ldots, (x_n, y_n)$ gives values $(x_i - y_i)$. The differences must be symmetrically distributed.
Two-sample tests for unpaired samples	Normal test for the difference in the means of two samples with common variance. N(0, 1)	The difference in the means of the two populations is $\mu_1 - \mu_2$. Special case: $\mu_1 = \mu_2$	$z = \dfrac{(\bar{x} - \bar{y}) - (\mu_1 - \mu_2)}{\sigma\sqrt{\frac{1}{n_1} + \frac{1}{n_2}}}$	Exact if $X \sim N(\mu_1, \sigma^2)$ and $Y \sim N(\mu_2, \sigma^2)$ (n.b. common known variance σ^2). Approximate if X and Y are not Normal (large samples required). Approximate if σ^2 has to be estimated (large samples required).
	Normal test for the difference in the means of two samples with different variances. N(0, 1)	The difference in the means of the two populations is $\mu_1 - \mu_2$. Special case: $\mu_1 = \mu_2$	$z = \dfrac{(\bar{x} - \bar{y}) - (\mu_1 - \mu_2)}{\sqrt{\frac{\sigma_1^2}{n_1} + \frac{\sigma_2^2}{n_2}}}$	Exact if $X \sim N(\mu_1, \sigma_1^2)$ and $Y \sim N(\mu_2, \sigma_2^2)$. Approximate if X and Y are not Normal (large samples required). If σ_1^2 and σ_2^2 are not known, they are estimated by s_1^2 and s_2^2 (large samples required).
	t test for the difference in the means of two samples $t_{n_1 + n_2 - 2}$	The difference in the means of two populations is $\mu_1 - \mu_2$. Special case: $\mu_1 = \mu_2$	$z = \dfrac{(\bar{x} - \bar{y}) - (\mu_1 - \mu_2)}{s\sqrt{\frac{1}{n_1} + \frac{1}{n_2}}}$	The populations are Normal, $X \sim N(\mu_1, \sigma^2)$ and $Y \sim N(\mu_2, \sigma^2)$ (n.b. common, unknown, variance σ^2). s^2 must be calculated as $\dfrac{(n_1 - 1)s_1^2 + (n_2 - 1)s_2^2}{n_1 + n_2 - 2}$
	Wilcoxon rank sum (or Mann–Whitney) two-sample test	The two samples are drawn from a common distribution.	Samples size $m, n : m \leq n$. Wilcoxon: W = sum of ranks of sample size m. Mann–Whitney: $T = W - \frac{1}{2}m(m+1)$ or $mn - \{W - \frac{1}{2}m(m+1)\}$ if smaller	H_1: the populations differ only in location parameter. Normal approximation for large m, n. For W: Mean $\frac{1}{2}mn + \frac{1}{2}m(m+1)$, Variance $\frac{1}{12}mn(m+n+1)$. For T: Mean $\frac{1}{2}mn$, Variance $\frac{1}{12}mn(m+n+1)$
	F test on ratio of two variances F_{n_1-1, n_2-1}	The ratio of the variances of the two populations is $\dfrac{\sigma_1^2}{\sigma_2^2}$. Special case: $\sigma_1^2 = \sigma_2^2$	$F = \dfrac{s_1^2/\sigma_1^2}{s_2^2/\sigma_2^2} \quad (s_1^2 > s_2^2)$	The populations are Normal: s_1^2 and s_2^2 must be calculated with divisors $(n_1 - 1)$ and $(n_2 - 1)$.

Statistics: Which test?

Which hypothesis test to use?

Although the table of hypothesis tests on pages 52 and 53 contains many commonly-used tests, including those taught at A level, there are some more specialised tests not included in it. The following decision trees will help you to select the most appropriate test, if it is in the table in this book.

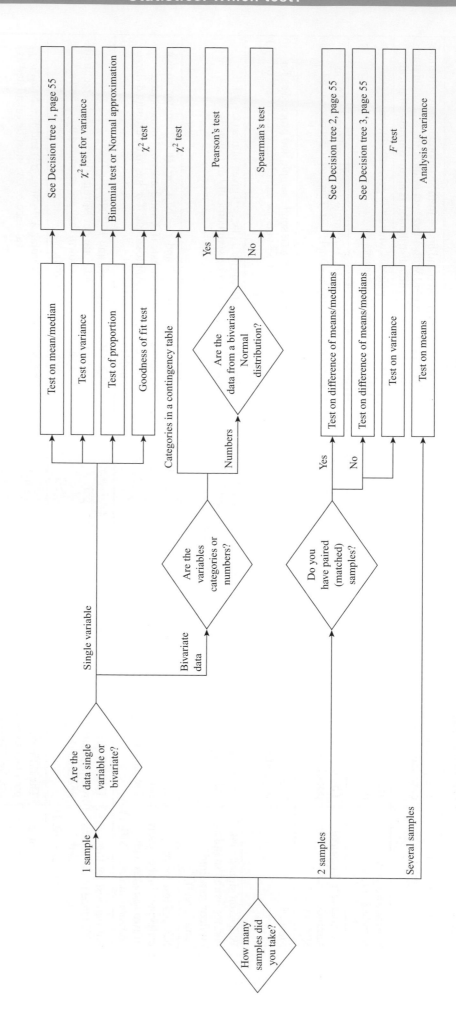

Statistics: Which test?

Decision tree 1: Tests on mean/median from a single sample

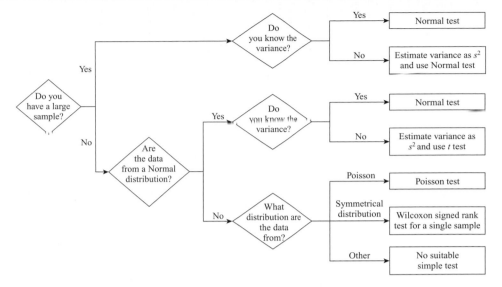

Decision tree 2: Tests on differences of means/medians from paired samples

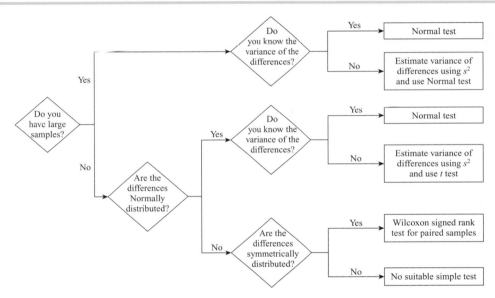

Decision tree 3: Tests on differences of means/medians from unpaired samples

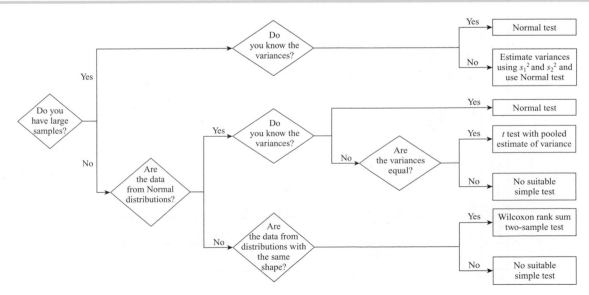

The binomial distribution: cumulative probabilities

$$P(X \le x) = \sum_{r=0}^{x} {}^{n}C_{r}(1-p)^{n-r}\,p^{r}$$

n	x	0.050	0.100	0.150	$\frac{1}{6}$	0.200	0.250	0.300	$\frac{1}{3}$	0.350	0.400	0.450	0.500	0.550	0.600	0.650	$\frac{2}{3}$	0.700	0.750	0.800	$\frac{5}{6}$	0.850	0.900	0.950
1	0	0.9500	0.9000	0.8500	0.8333	0.8000	0.7500	0.7000	0.6667	0.6500	0.6000	0.5500	0.5000	0.4500	0.4000	0.3500	0.3333	0.3000	0.2500	0.2000	0.1667	0.1500	0.1000	0.0500
	1	1.0000	1.0000	1.0000	1.0000	1.0000	1.0000	1.0000	1.0000	1.0000	1.0000	1.0000	1.0000	1.0000	1.0000	1.0000	1.0000	1.0000	1.0000	1.0000	1.0000	1.0000	1.0000	1.0000
2	0	0.9025	0.8100	0.7225	0.6944	0.6400	0.5625	0.4900	0.4444	0.4225	0.3600	0.3025	0.2500	0.2025	0.1600	0.1225	0.1111	0.0900	0.0625	0.0400	0.0278	0.0225	0.0100	0.0025
	1	0.9975	0.9900	0.9775	0.9722	0.9600	0.9375	0.9100	0.8889	0.8775	0.8400	0.7975	0.7500	0.6975	0.6400	0.5775	0.5556	0.5100	0.4375	0.3600	0.3056	0.2775	0.1900	0.0975
	2	1.0000	1.0000	1.0000	1.0000	1.0000	1.0000	1.0000	1.0000	1.0000	1.0000	1.0000	1.0000	1.0000	1.0000	1.0000	1.0000	1.0000	1.0000	1.0000	1.0000	1.0000	1.0000	1.0000
3	0	0.8574	0.7290	0.6141	0.5787	0.5120	0.4219	0.3430	0.2963	0.2746	0.2160	0.1664	0.1250	0.0911	0.0640	0.0429	0.0370	0.0270	0.0156	0.0080	0.0046	0.0034	0.0010	0.0001
	1	0.9928	0.9720	0.9392	0.9259	0.8960	0.8437	0.7840	0.7407	0.7183	0.6480	0.5748	0.5000	0.4252	0.3520	0.2818	0.2593	0.2160	0.1563	0.1040	0.0741	0.0608	0.0280	0.0073
	2	0.9999	0.9990	0.9966	0.9954	0.9920	0.9844	0.9730	0.9630	0.9571	0.9360	0.9089	0.8750	0.8336	0.7840	0.7254	0.7037	0.6570	0.5781	0.4880	0.4213	0.3859	0.2710	0.1426
	3	1.0000	1.0000	1.0000	1.0000	1.0000	1.0000	1.0000	1.0000	1.0000	1.0000	1.0000	1.0000	1.0000	1.0000	1.0000	1.0000	1.0000	1.0000	1.0000	1.0000	1.0000	1.0000	1.0000
4	0	0.8145	0.6561	0.5220	0.4823	0.4096	0.3164	0.2401	0.1975	0.1785	0.1296	0.0915	0.0625	0.0410	0.0256	0.0150	0.0123	0.0081	0.0039	0.0016	0.0008	0.0005	0.0001	0.0000
	1	0.9860	0.9477	0.8905	0.8681	0.8192	0.7383	0.6517	0.5926	0.5630	0.4752	0.3910	0.3125	0.2415	0.1792	0.1265	0.1111	0.0837	0.0508	0.0272	0.0162	0.0120	0.0037	0.0005
	2	0.9995	0.9963	0.9880	0.9838	0.9728	0.9492	0.9163	0.8889	0.8735	0.8208	0.7585	0.6875	0.6090	0.5248	0.4370	0.4074	0.3483	0.2617	0.1808	0.1319	0.1095	0.0523	0.0140
	3	1.0000	0.9999	0.9995	0.9992	0.9984	0.9961	0.9919	0.9877	0.9850	0.9744	0.9590	0.9375	0.9085	0.8704	0.8215	0.8025	0.7599	0.6836	0.5904	0.5177	0.4780	0.3439	0.1855
	4		1.0000	1.0000	1.0000	1.0000	1.0000	1.0000	1.0000	1.0000	1.0000	1.0000	1.0000	1.0000	1.0000	1.0000	1.0000	1.0000	1.0000	1.0000	1.0000	1.0000	1.0000	1.0000
5	0	0.7738	0.5905	0.4437	0.4019	0.3277	0.2373	0.1681	0.1317	0.1160	0.0778	0.0503	0.0313	0.0185	0.0102	0.0053	0.0041	0.0024	0.0010	0.0003	0.0001	0.0001	0.0000	0.0000
	1	0.9774	0.9185	0.8352	0.8038	0.7373	0.6328	0.5282	0.4609	0.4284	0.3370	0.2562	0.1875	0.1312	0.0870	0.0540	0.0453	0.0308	0.0156	0.0067	0.0033	0.0022	0.0005	0.0000
	2	0.9988	0.9914	0.9734	0.9645	0.9421	0.8965	0.8369	0.7901	0.7648	0.6826	0.5931	0.5000	0.4069	0.3174	0.2352	0.2099	0.1631	0.1035	0.0579	0.0355	0.0266	0.0086	0.0012
	3	1.0000	0.9995	0.9978	0.9967	0.9933	0.9844	0.9692	0.9547	0.9460	0.9130	0.8688	0.8125	0.7438	0.6630	0.5716	0.5391	0.4718	0.3672	0.2627	0.1962	0.1648	0.0815	0.0226
	4		1.0000	0.9999	0.9999	0.9997	0.9990	0.9976	0.9959	0.9947	0.9898	0.9815	0.9688	0.9497	0.9222	0.8840	0.8683	0.8319	0.7627	0.6723	0.5981	0.5563	0.4095	0.2262
	5		1.0000	1.0000	1.0000	1.0000	1.0000	1.0000	1.0000	1.0000	1.0000	1.0000	1.0000	1.0000	1.0000	1.0000	1.0000	1.0000	1.0000	1.0000	1.0000	1.0000	1.0000	1.0000
6	0	0.7351	0.5314	0.3771	0.3349	0.2621	0.1780	0.1176	0.0878	0.0754	0.0467	0.0277	0.0156	0.0083	0.0041	0.0018	0.0014	0.0007	0.0002	0.0001	0.0000	0.0000	0.0000	0.0000
	1	0.9672	0.8857	0.7765	0.7368	0.6554	0.5339	0.4202	0.3512	0.3191	0.2333	0.1636	0.1094	0.0692	0.0410	0.0223	0.0178	0.0109	0.0046	0.0016	0.0007	0.0004	0.0001	0.0000
	2	0.9978	0.9841	0.9527	0.9377	0.9011	0.8306	0.7443	0.6804	0.6471	0.5443	0.4415	0.3438	0.2553	0.1792	0.1174	0.1001	0.0705	0.0376	0.0170	0.0087	0.0059	0.0013	0.0001
	3	0.9999	0.9987	0.9941	0.9913	0.9830	0.9624	0.9295	0.8999	0.8826	0.8208	0.7447	0.6563	0.5585	0.4557	0.3529	0.3196	0.2557	0.1694	0.0989	0.0623	0.0473	0.0159	0.0022
	4	1.0000	0.9999	0.9996	0.9993	0.9984	0.9954	0.9891	0.9822	0.9777	0.9590	0.9308	0.8906	0.8364	0.7667	0.6809	0.6488	0.5798	0.4661	0.3446	0.2632	0.2235	0.1143	0.0328
	5		1.0000	1.0000	1.0000	0.9999	0.9998	0.9993	0.9986	0.9982	0.9959	0.9917	0.9844	0.9723	0.9533	0.9246	0.9122	0.8824	0.8220	0.7379	0.6651	0.6229	0.4686	0.2649
	6		1.0000	1.0000	1.0000	1.0000	1.0000	1.0000	1.0000	1.0000	1.0000	1.0000	1.0000	1.0000	1.0000	1.0000	1.0000	1.0000	1.0000	1.0000	1.0000	1.0000	1.0000	1.0000
7	0	0.6983	0.4783	0.3206	0.2791	0.2097	0.1335	0.0824	0.0585	0.0490	0.0280	0.0152	0.0078	0.0037	0.0016	0.0006	0.0005	0.0002	0.0001	0.0000	0.0000	0.0000	0.0000	0.0000
	1	0.9556	0.8503	0.7166	0.6698	0.5767	0.4449	0.3294	0.2634	0.2338	0.1586	0.1024	0.0625	0.0357	0.0188	0.0090	0.0069	0.0038	0.0013	0.0004	0.0001	0.0001	0.0000	0.0000
	2	0.9962	0.9743	0.9262	0.9042	0.8520	0.7564	0.6471	0.5706	0.5323	0.4199	0.3164	0.2266	0.1529	0.0963	0.0556	0.0453	0.0288	0.0129	0.0047	0.0020	0.0012	0.0002	0.0000
	3	0.9998	0.9973	0.9879	0.9824	0.9667	0.9294	0.8740	0.8267	0.8002	0.7102	0.6083	0.5000	0.3917	0.2898	0.1998	0.1733	0.1260	0.0706	0.0333	0.0176	0.0121	0.0027	0.0002
	4	1.0000	0.9998	0.9988	0.9980	0.9953	0.9871	0.9712	0.9547	0.9444	0.9037	0.8471	0.7734	0.6836	0.5801	0.4677	0.4294	0.3529	0.2436	0.1480	0.0958	0.0738	0.0257	0.0038
	5	1.0000	1.0000	0.9999	0.9999	0.9996	0.9987	0.9962	0.9931	0.9910	0.9812	0.9643	0.9375	0.8976	0.8414	0.7662	0.7366	0.6706	0.5551	0.4233	0.3302	0.2834	0.1497	0.0444
	6		1.0000	1.0000	1.0000	1.0000	0.9999	0.9998	0.9995	0.9994	0.9984	0.9963	0.9922	0.9848	0.9720	0.9510	0.9415	0.9176	0.8665	0.7903	0.7209	0.6794	0.5217	0.3017
	7		1.0000	1.0000	1.0000	1.0000	1.0000	1.0000	1.0000	1.0000	1.0000	1.0000	1.0000	1.0000	1.0000	1.0000	1.0000	1.0000	1.0000	1.0000	1.0000	1.0000	1.0000	1.0000

The binomial distribution: cumulative probabilities

n	x \ p	0.050	0.100	0.150	$\frac{1}{6}$	0.200	0.250	0.300	$\frac{1}{3}$	0.350	0.400	0.450	0.500	0.550	0.600	0.650	$\frac{2}{3}$	0.700	0.750	0.800	$\frac{5}{6}$	0.850	0.900	0.950
8	0	0.6634	0.4305	0.2725	0.2326	0.1678	0.1001	0.0576	0.0390	0.0319	0.0168	0.0084	0.0039	0.0017	0.0007	0.0002	0.0002	0.0001	0.0000	0.0000				
	1	0.9428	0.8131	0.6572	0.6047	0.5033	0.3671	0.2553	0.1951	0.1691	0.1064	0.0632	0.0352	0.0181	0.0085	0.0036	0.0026	0.0013	0.0004	0.0001	0.0000	0.0000		
	2	0.9942	0.9619	0.8948	0.8652	0.7969	0.6785	0.5518	0.4682	0.4278	0.3154	0.2201	0.1445	0.0885	0.0498	0.0253	0.0197	0.0113	0.0042	0.0012	0.0004	0.0002	0.0000	
	3	0.9996	0.9950	0.9786	0.9693	0.9437	0.8862	0.8059	0.7414	0.7064	0.5941	0.4770	0.3633	0.2604	0.1737	0.1061	0.0879	0.0580	0.0273	0.0104	0.0046	0.0029	0.0004	0.0000
	4	1.0000	0.9996	0.9971	0.9954	0.9896	0.9727	0.9420	0.9121	0.8939	0.8263	0.7396	0.6367	0.5230	0.4059	0.2936	0.2587	0.1941	0.1138	0.0563	0.0307	0.0214	0.0050	0.0004
	5		1.0000	0.9998	0.9996	0.9988	0.9958	0.9887	0.9803	0.9747	0.9502	0.9115	0.8555	0.7799	0.6846	0.5722	0.5318	0.4482	0.3215	0.2031	0.1348	0.1052	0.0381	0.0058
	6			1.0000	1.0000	0.9999	0.9996	0.9987	0.9974	0.9964	0.9915	0.9819	0.9648	0.9368	0.8936	0.8309	0.8049	0.7447	0.6329	0.4967	0.3953	0.3428	0.1869	0.0572
	7					1.0000	1.0000	0.9999	0.9998	0.9998	0.9993	0.9983	0.9961	0.9916	0.9832	0.9681	0.9610	0.9424	0.8999	0.8322	0.7674	0.7275	0.5695	0.3366
	8							1.0000	1.0000	1.0000	1.0000	1.0000	1.0000	1.0000	1.0000	1.0000	1.0000	1.0000	1.0000	1.0000	1.0000	1.0000	1.0000	1.0000
9	0	0.6302	0.3874	0.2316	0.1938	0.1342	0.0751	0.0404	0.0260	0.0207	0.0101	0.0046	0.0020	0.0008	0.0003	0.0001	0.0001	0.0000	00000					
	1	0.9288	0.7748	0.5995	0.5427	0.4362	0.3003	0.1960	0.1431	0.1211	0.0705	0.0385	0.0195	0.0091	0.0038	0.0014	0.0010	0.0004	0.0001	0.0000	0.0000			
	2	0.9916	0.9470	0.8591	0.8217	0.7382	0.6007	0.4628	0.3772	0.3373	0.2318	0.1495	0.0898	0.0498	0.0250	0.0112	0.0083	0.0043	0.0013	0.0003	0.0001	0.0000	0.0000	
	3	0.9994	0.9917	0.9661	0.9520	0.9144	0.8343	0.7297	0.6503	0.6089	0.4826	0.3614	0.2539	0.1658	0.0994	0.0536	0.0424	0.0253	0.0100	0.0031	0.0011	0.0006	0.0001	
	4	1.0000	0.9991	0.9944	0.9911	0.9804	0.9511	0.9012	0.8552	0.8283	0.7334	0.6214	0.5000	0.3786	0.2666	0.1717	0.1448	0.0988	0.0489	0.0196	0.0090	0.0056	0.0009	0.0000
	5		0.9999	0.9994	0.9989	0.9969	0.9900	0.9747	0.9576	0.9464	0.9006	0.8342	0.7461	0.6386	0.5174	0.3911	0.3497	0.2703	0.1657	0.0856	0.0480	0.0339	0.0083	0.0006
	6		1.0000	1.0000	0.9999	0.9997	0.9987	0.9957	0.9917	0.9888	0.9750	0.9502	0.9102	0.8505	0.7682	0.6627	0.6228	0.5372	0.3993	0.2618	0.1783	0.1409	0.0530	0.0084
	7				1.0000	1.0000	0.9999	0.9996	0.9990	0.9986	0.9962	0.9909	0.9805	0.9615	0.9295	0.8789	0.8569	0.8040	0.6997	0.5638	0.4573	0.4005	0.2252	0.0712
	8						1.0000	1.0000	0.9999	0.9999	0.9997	0.9992	0.9980	09954	0.9899	0.9793	0.9740	0.9596	0.9249	0.8658	0.8062	0.7684	0.6126	0.3698
	9								1.0000	1.0000	1.0000	1.0000	1.0000	1.0000	1.0000	1.0000	1.0000	1.0000	1.0000	1.0000	1.0000	1.0000	1.0000	1.0000
10	0	0.5987	0.3487	0.1969	0.1615	0.1074	0.0563	0.0282	0.0173	0.0135	0.0060	0.0025	0.0010	0.0003	0.0001	0.0000	0.0000	0.0000						
	1	0.9139	0.7361	0.5443	0.4845	0.3758	0.2440	0.1493	0.1040	0.0860	0.0464	0.0233	0.0107	0.0045	0.0017	0.0005	0.0004	0.0001	0.0000	0.0000				
	2	0.9885	0.9298	0.8202	0.7752	0.6778	0.5256	0.3828	0.2991	0.2616	0.1673	0.0996	0.0547	0.0274	0.0123	0.0048	0.0034	0.0016	0.0004	0.0001	0.0000	0.0000		
	3	0.9990	0.9872	0.9500	0.9303	0.8791	0.7759	0.6496	0.5593	0.5138	0.3823	0.2660	0.1719	0.1020	0.0548	0.0260	0.0197	0.0106	0.0035	0.0009	0.0003	0.0001	0.0000	
	4	0.9999	0.9984	0.9901	0.9845	0.9672	0.9219	0.8497	0.7869	0.7515	0.6331	0.5044	0.3770	0.2616	0.1662	0.0949	0.0766	0.0473	0.0197	0.0064	0.0024	0.0014	0.0001	0.0000
	5	1.0000	0.9999	0.9986	0.9976	0.9936	0.9803	0.9527	0.9234	0.9051	0.8338	0.7384	0.6230	0.4956	0.3669	0.2485	0.2131	0.1503	0.0781	0.0328	0.0155	0.0099	0.0016	0.0001
	6		1.0000	0.9999	0.9997	0.9991	0.9965	0.9894	0.9803	0.9740	0.9452	0.8980	0.8281	0.7340	0.6177	0.4862	0.4407	0.3504	0.2241	0.1209	0.0697	0.0500	0.0128	0.0010
	7			1.0000	1.0000	0.9999	0.9996	0.9984	0.9966	0.9952	0.9877	0.9726	0.9453	0.9004	0.8327	0.7384	0.7009	0.6172	0.4744	0.3222	0.2248	0.1798	0.0702	0.0115
	8					1.0000	1.0000	0.9999	0.9996	0.9995	0.9983	0.9955	0.9893	0.9767	0.9536	0.9140	0.8960	0.8507	0.7560	0.6242	0.5155	0.4557	0.2639	0.0861
	9							1.0000	1.0000	1.0000	0.9999	0.9997	0.9990	0.9975	0.9940	0.9865	0.9827	0.9718	0.9437	0.8926	0.8385	0.8031	0.6513	0.4013
	10										1.0000	1.0000	1.0000	1.0000	1.0000	1.0000	1.0000	1.0000	1.0000	1.0000	1.0000	1.0000	1.0000	1.0000
11	0	0.5688	0.3138	0.1673	0.1346	0.0859	0.0422	0.0198	0.0116	0.0088	0.0036	0.0014	0.0005	0.0002	0.0000	0.0000	0.0000							
	1	0.8981	0.6974	0.4922	0.4307	0.3221	0.1971	0.1130	0.0751	0.0606	0.0302	0.0139	0.0059	0.0022	0.0007	0.0002	0.0001	0.0000	0.0000					
	2	0.9848	0.9104	0.7788	0.7268	0.6174	0.4552	0.3127	0.2341	0.2001	0.1189	0.0652	0.0327	0.0148	0.0059	0.0020	0.0014	0.0006	0.0001	0.0000	0.0000			
	3	0.9984	0.9815	0.9306	0.9044	0.8389	0.7133	0.5696	0.4726	0.4256	0.2963	0.1911	0.1133	0.0610	0.0293	0.0122	0.0088	0.0043	0.0012	0.0002	0.0000	0.0000		
	4	0.9999	0.9972	0.9841	0.9755	0.9496	0.8854	0.7897	0.7110	0.6683	0.5328	0.3971	0.2744	0.1738	0.0994	0.0501	0.0386	0.0216	0.0076	0.0020	0.0006	0.0003	0.0000	
	5	1.0000	0.9997	0.9973	0.9954	0.9883	0.9657	0.9218	0.8779	0.8513	0.7535	0.6331	0.5000	0.3669	0.2465	0.1487	0.1221	0.0782	0.0343	0.0117	0.0046	0.0027	0.0003	0.0000
	6		1.0000	0.9997	0.9994	0.9980	0.9924	0.9784	0.9614	0.9499	0.9006	0.8262	0.7256	0.6029	0.4672	0.3317	0.2890	0.2103	0.1146	0.0504	0.0245	0.0159	0.0028	0.0001
	7			1.0000	0.9999	0.9998	0.9988	0.9957	0.9912	0.9878	0.9707	0.9390	0.8867	0.8089	0.7037	0.5744	0.5274	0.4304	0.2867	0.1611	0.0956	0.0694	0.0185	0.0016
	8				1.0000	1.0000	0.9999	0.9994	0.9986	0.9980	0.9941	0.9852	0.9673	0.9348	0.8811	0.7999	0.7659	0.6873	0.5448	0.3826	0.2732	0.2212	0.0896	0.0152
	9						1.0000	1.0000	0.9999	0.9998	0.9993	0.9978	0.9941	0.9861	0.9698	0.9394	0.9249	0.8870	0.8029	0.6779	0.5693	0.5078	0.3026	0.1019
	10								1.0000	1.0000	1.0000	0.9998	0.9995	0.9986	0.9964	0.9912	0.9884	0.9802	0.9578	0.9141	0.8654	0.8327	0.6862	0.4312
	11											1.0000	1.0000	1.0000	1.0000	1.0000	1.0000	1.0000	1.0000	1.0000	1.0000	1.0000	1.0000	1.0000

The binomial distribution: cumulative probabilities

n	x	0.050	0.100	0.150	$\frac{1}{6}$	0.200	0.250	0.300	$\frac{1}{3}$	0.350	0.400	0.450	0.500	0.550	0.600	0.650	$\frac{2}{3}$	0.700	0.750	0.800	$\frac{5}{6}$	0.850	0.900	0.950
12	0	0.5404	0.2824	0.1422	0.1122	0.0687	0.0317	0.0138	0.0077	0.0057	0.0022	0.0008	0.0002	0.0001	0.0000	0.0000								
	1	0.8816	0.6590	0.4435	0.3813	0.2749	0.1584	0.0850	0.0540	0.0424	0.0196	0.0083	0.0032	0.0011	0.0003	0.0001	0.0000	0.0000						
	2	0.9804	0.8891	0.7358	0.6774	0.5583	0.3907	0.2528	0.1811	0.1513	0.0834	0.0421	0.0193	0.0079	0.0028	0.0008	0.0005	0.0002	0.0000	0.0000				
	3	0.9978	0.9744	0.9078	0.8748	0.7946	0.6488	0.4925	0.3931	0.3467	0.2253	0.1345	0.0730	0.0356	0.0153	0.0056	0.0039	0.0017	0.0004	0.0001	0.0000	0.0000		
	4	0.9998	0.9957	0.9761	0.9637	0.9274	0.8424	0.7237	0.6315	0.5833	0.4382	0.3044	0.1938	0.1117	0.0573	0.0255	0.0188	0.0095	0.0028	0.0006	0.0002	0.0001	0.0000	
	5	1.0000	0.9995	0.9954	0.9921	0.9806	0.9456	0.8822	0.8223	0.7873	0.6652	0.5269	0.3872	0.2607	0.1582	0.0846	0.0664	0.0386	0.0143	0.0039	0.0013	0.0007	0.0001	
	6		0.9999	0.9993	0.9987	0.9961	0.9857	0.9614	0.9336	0.9154	0.8418	0.7393	0.6128	0.4731	0.3348	0.2127	0.1777	0.1178	0.0544	0.0194	0.0079	0.0046	0.0005	0.0000
	7		1.0000	0.9999	0.9998	0.9994	0.9972	0.9905	0.9812	0.9745	0.9427	0.8883	0.8062	0.6956	0.5618	0.4167	0.3685	0.2763	0.1576	0.0726	0.0364	0.0239	0.0043	0.0002
	8			1.0000	1.0000	0.9999	0.9996	0.9983	0.9961	0.9944	0.9847	0.9644	0.9270	0.8655	0.7747	0.6533	0.6069	0.5075	0.3512	0.2054	0.1252	0.0922	0.0256	0.0022
	9					1.0000	1.0000	0.9998	0.9995	0.9992	0.9972	0.9921	0.9807	0.9579	0.9166	0.8487	0.8189	0.7472	0.6093	0.4417	0.3226	0.2642	0.1109	0.0196
	10							1.0000	1.0000	0.9999	0.9997	0.9989	0.9968	0.9917	0.9804	0.9576	0.9460	0.9150	0.8416	0.7251	0.6187	0.5565	0.3410	0.1184
	11									1.0000	1.0000	0.9999	0.9998	0.9992	0.9978	0.9943	0.9923	0.9862	0.9683	0.9313	0.8878	0.8578	0.7176	0.4596
	12											1.0000	1.0000	1.0000	1.0000	1.0000	1.0000	1.0000	1.0000	1.0000	1.0000	1.0000	1.0000	1.0000
13	0	0.5133	0.2542	0.1209	0.0935	0.0550	0.0238	0.0097	0.0051	0.0037	0.0013	0.0004	0.0001	0.0000	0.0000									
	1	0.8646	0.6213	0.3983	0.3365	0.2336	0.1267	0.0637	0.0385	0.0296	0.0126	0.0049	0.0017	0.0005	0.0001	0.0000	0.0000	0.0000						
	2	0.9755	0.8661	0.6920	0.6281	0.5017	0.3326	0.2025	0.1387	0.1132	0.0579	0.0269	0.0112	0.0041	0.0013	0.0003	0.0002	0.0001	0.0000					
	3	0.9969	0.9658	0.8820	0.8419	0.7473	0.5843	0.4206	0.3224	0.2783	0.1686	0.0929	0.0461	0.0203	0.0078	0.0025	0.0016	0.0007	0.0001	0.0000				
	4	0.9997	0.9935	0.9658	0.9488	0.9009	0.7940	0.6543	0.5520	0.5005	0.3530	0.2279	0.1334	0.0698	0.0321	0.0126	0.0088	0.0040	0.0010	0.0002	0.0000	0.0000		
	5	1.0000	0.9991	0.9925	0.9873	0.9700	0.9198	0.8346	0.7587	0.7159	0.5744	0.4268	0.2905	0.1788	0.0977	0.0462	0.0347	0.0182	0.0056	0.0012	0.0003	0.0002	0.0000	
	6		0.9999	0.9987	0.9976	0.9930	0.9757	0.9376	0.8965	0.8705	0.7712	0.6437	0.5000	0.3563	0.2288	0.1295	0.1035	0.0624	0.0243	0.0070	0.0024	0.0013	0.0001	
	7		1.0000	0.9998	0.9997	0.9988	0.9944	0.9818	0.9653	0.9538	0.9023	0.8212	0.7095	0.5732	0.4256	0.2841	0.2413	0.1654	0.0802	0.0300	0.0127	0.0075	0.0009	0.0000
	8			1.0000	1.0000	0.9998	0.9990	0.9960	0.9912	0.9874	0.9679	0.9302	0.8666	0.7721	0.6470	0.4995	0.4480	0.3457	0.2060	0.0991	0.0512	0.0342	0.0065	0.0003
	9					1.0000	0.9999	0.9993	0.9984	0.9975	0.9922	0.9797	0.9539	0.9071	0.8314	0.7217	0.6776	0.5794	0.4157	0.2527	0.1581	0.1180	0.0342	0.0031
	10						1.0000	0.9999	0.9998	0.9997	0.9987	0.9959	0.9888	0.9731	0.9421	0.8868	0.8613	0.7975	0.6674	0.4983	0.3719	0.3080	0.1339	0.0245
	11							1.0000	1.0000	1.0000	0.9999	0.9995	0.9983	0.9951	0.9874	0.9704	0.9615	0.9363	0.8733	0.7664	0.6635	0.6017	0.3787	0.1354
	12										1.0000	1.0000	0.9999	0.9996	0.9987	0.9963	0.9949	0.9903	0.9762	0.9450	0.9065	0.8791	0.7458	0.4867
	13												1.0000	1.0000	1.0000	1.0000	1.0000	1.0000	1.0000	1.0000	1.0000	1.0000	1.0000	1.0000
14	0	0.4877	0.2288	0.1028	0.0779	0.0440	0.0178	0.0068	0.0034	0.0024	0.0008	0.0002	0.0001	0.0000	0.0000									
	1	0.8470	0.5846	0.3567	0.2960	0.1979	0.1010	0.0475	0.0274	0.0205	0.0081	0.0029	0.0009	0.0003	0.0001	0.0000	0.0000							
	2	0.9699	0.8416	0.6479	0.5795	0.4481	0.2811	0.1608	0.1053	0.0839	0.0398	0.0170	0.0065	0.0022	0.0006	0.0001	0.0001	0.0000						
	3	0.9958	0.9559	0.8535	0.8063	0.6982	0.5213	0.3552	0.2612	0.2205	0.1243	0.0632	0.0287	0.0114	0.0039	0.0011	0.0007	0.0002	0.0000					
	4	0.9996	0.9908	0.9533	0.9310	0.8702	0.7415	0.5842	0.4755	0.4227	0.2793	0.1672	0.0898	0.0426	0.0175	0.0060	0.0040	0.0017	0.0003	0.0000	0.0000			
	5	1.0000	0.9985	0.9885	0.9809	0.9561	0.8883	0.7805	0.6898	0.6405	0.4859	0.3373	0.2120	0.1189	0.0583	0.0243	0.0174	0.0083	0.0022	0.0004	0.0001	0.0000		
	6		0.9998	0.9978	0.9959	0.9884	0.9617	0.9067	0.8505	0.8164	0.6925	0.5461	0.3953	0.2586	0.1501	0.0753	0.0576	0.0315	0.0103	0.0024	0.0007	0.0003	0.0000	
	7		1.0000	0.9997	0.9993	0.9976	0.9897	0.9685	0.9424	0.9247	0.8499	0.7414	0.6047	0.4539	0.3075	0.1836	0.1495	0.0933	0.0383	0.0116	0.0041	0.0022	0.0002	0.0000
	8			1.0000	0.9999	0.9996	0.9978	0.9917	0.9826	0.9757	0.9417	0.8811	0.7880	0.6627	0.5141	0.3595	0.3102	0.2195	0.1117	0.0439	0.0191	0.0115	0.0015	0.0000
	9				1.0000	1.0000	0.9997	0.9983	0.9960	0.9940	0.9825	0.9574	0.9102	0.8328	0.7207	0.5773	0.5245	0.4158	0.2585	0.1298	0.0690	0.0467	0.0092	0.0004
	10						1.0000	0.9998	0.9993	0.9989	0.9961	0.9886	0.9713	0.9368	0.8757	0.7795	0.7388	0.6448	0.4787	0.3018	0.1937	0.1465	0.0441	0.0042
	11							1.0000	0.9999	0.9999	0.9994	0.9978	0.9935	0.9830	0.9602	0.9161	0.8947	0.8392	0.7189	0.5519	0.4205	0.3521	0.1584	0.0301
	12								1.0000	1.0000	0.9999	0.9997	0.9991	0.9971	0.9919	0.9795	0.9726	0.9525	0.8990	0.8021	0.7040	0.6433	0.4154	0.1530
	13										1.0000	1.0000	0.9999	0.9998	0.9992	0.9976	0.9966	0.9932	0.9822	0.9560	0.9221	0.8972	0.7712	0.5123
	14												1.0000	1.0000	1.0000	1.0000	1.0000	1.0000	1.0000	1.0000	1.0000	1.0000	1.0000	1.0000

The binomial distribution: cumulative probabilities

n	x	0.050	0.100	0.150	1/6	0.200	0.250	0.300	1/3	0.350	0.400	0.450	0.500	0.550	0.600	0.650	2/3	0.700	0.750	0.800	5/6	0.850	0.900	0.950
15	0	0.4633	0.2059	0.0874	0.0649	0.0352	0.0134	0.0047	0.0023	0.0016	0.0005	0.0001	0.0000	0.0000										
	1	0.8290	0.5490	0.3186	0.2596	0.1671	0.0802	0.0353	0.0194	0.0142	0.0052	0.0017	0.0005	0.0001	0.0000	0.0000								
	2	0.9638	0.8159	0.6042	0.5322	0.3980	0.2361	0.1268	0.0794	0.0617	0.0271	0.0107	0.0037	0.0011	0.0003	0.0001	0.0000							
	3	0.9945	0.9444	0.8227	0.7685	0.6482	0.4613	0.2969	0.2092	0.1727	0.0905	0.0424	0.0176	0.0063	0.0019	0.0005	0.0003	0.0000	0.0000					
	4	0.9994	0.9873	0.9383	0.9102	0.8358	0.6865	0.5155	0.4041	0.3519	0.2173	0.1204	0.0592	0.0255	0.0093	0.0028	0.0018	0.0001	0.0001	0.0000				
	5	0.9999	0.9978	0.9832	0.9726	0.9389	0.8516	0.7216	0.6184	0.5643	0.4032	0.2608	0.1509	0.0769	0.0338	0.0124	0.0085	0.0037	0.0008	0.0001	0.0000	0.0000		
	6	1.0000	0.9997	0.9964	0.9934	0.9819	0.9434	0.8689	0.7970	0.7548	0.6098	0.4522	0.3036	0.1818	0.0950	0.0422	0.0308	0.0152	0.0042	0.0008	0.0002	0.0001		
	7		1.0000	0.9994	0.9987	0.9958	0.9827	0.9500	0.9118	0.8868	0.7869	0.6535	0.5000	0.3465	0.2131	0.1132	0.0882	0.0500	0.0173	0.0042	0.0013	0.0006	0.0000	
	8			0.9999	0.9998	0.9992	0.9958	0.9848	0.9692	0.9578	0.9050	0.8182	0.6964	0.5478	0.3902	0.2452	0.2030	0.1311	0.0566	0.0181	0.0066	0.0036	0.0003	0.0000
	9			1.0000	1.0000	0.9999	0.9992	0.9963	0.9915	0.9876	0.9662	0.9231	0.8491	0.7392	0.5968	0.4357	0.3816	0.2784	0.1484	0.0611	0.0274	0.0168	0.0022	0.0001
	10					1.0000	0.9999	0.9993	0.9982	0.9972	0.9907	0.9745	0.9408	0.8796	0.7827	0.6481	0.5959	0.4845	0.3135	0.1642	0.0898	0.0617	0.0127	0.0006
	11						1.0000	0.9999	0.9997	0.9995	0.9981	0.9937	0.9824	0.9576	0.9095	0.8273	0.7908	0.7031	0.5387	0.3518	0.2315	0.1773	0.0556	0.0055
	12							1.0000	1.0000	0.9999	0.9997	0.9989	0.9963	0.9893	0.9729	0.9383	0.9206	0.8732	0.7639	0.6020	0.4678	0.3958	0.1841	0.0362
	13									1.0000	1.0000	0.9999	0.9995	0.9983	0.9948	0.9858	0.9806	0.9647	0.9198	0.8329	0.7404	0.6814	0.4510	0.1710
	14											1.0000	1.0000	0.9999	0.9995	0.9984	0.9977	0.9953	0.9866	0.9648	0.9351	0.9126	0.7941	0.5367
	15													1.0000	1.0000	1.0000	1.0000	1.0000	1.0000	1.0000	1.0000	1.0000	1.0000	1.0000
16	0	0.4401	0.1853	0.0743	0.0541	0.0281	0.0100	0.0033	0.0015	0.0010	0.0003	0.0001	0.0000	0.0000										
	1	0.8108	0.5147	0.2839	0.2272	0.1407	0.0635	0.0261	0.0137	0.0098	0.0033	0.0010	0.0003	0.0001	0.0000									
	2	0.9571	0.7892	0.5614	0.4868	0.3518	0.1971	0.0994	0.0594	0.0451	0.0183	0.0066	0.0021	0.0006	0.0001	0.0000	0.0000							
	3	0.9930	0.9316	0.7899	0.7291	0.5981	0.4050	0.2459	0.1659	0.1339	0.0651	0.0281	0.0106	0.0035	0.0009	0.0002	0.0001	0.0000						
	4	0.9991	0.9830	0.9209	0.8866	0.7982	0.6302	0.4499	0.3391	0.2892	0.1666	0.0853	0.0384	0.0149	0.0049	0.0013	0.0008	0.0003	0.0000					
	5	0.9999	0.9967	0.9765	0.9622	0.9183	0.8103	0.6598	0.5469	0.4900	0.3288	0.1976	0.1051	0.0486	0.0191	0.0062	0.0040	0.0016	0.0003	0.0000				
	6	1.0000	0.9995	0.9944	0.9899	0.9733	0.9204	0.8247	0.7374	0.6881	0.5272	0.3660	0.2272	0.1241	0.0583	0.0229	0.0159	0.0071	0.0016	0.0002	0.0000	0.0000		
	7		0.9999	0.9989	0.9979	0.9930	0.9729	0.9256	0.8735	0.8406	0.7161	0.5629	0.4018	0.2559	0.1423	0.0671	0.0500	0.0257	0.0075	0.0015	0.0004	0.0002	0.0000	
	8		1.0000	0.9998	0.9996	0.9985	0.9925	0.9743	0.9500	0.9329	0.8577	0.7441	0.5982	0.4371	0.2839	0.1594	0.1265	0.0744	0.0271	0.0070	0.0021	0.0011	0.0001	
	9			1.0000	1.0000	0.9998	0.9984	0.9929	0.9841	0.9771	0.9417	0.8759	0.7728	0.6340	0.4728	0.3119	0.2626	0.1753	0.0796	0.0267	0.0101	0.0056	0.0005	0.0000
	10					1.0000	0.9997	0.9984	0.9960	0.9938	0.9809	0.9514	0.8949	0.8024	0.6712	0.5100	0.4531	0.3402	0.1897	0.0817	0.0373	0.0235	0.0033	0.0001
	11						1.0000	0.9997	0.9992	0.9987	0.9951	0.9851	0.9616	0.9147	0.8334	0.7108	0.6609	0.5501	0.3698	0.2018	0.1134	0.0791	0.0170	0.0009
	12							1.0000	0.9999	0.9998	0.9991	0.9965	0.9894	0.9719	0.9349	0.8661	0.8341	0.7541	0.5950	0.4019	0.2709	0.2101	0.0684	0.0070
	13								1.0000	1.0000	0.9999	0.9994	0.9979	0.9934	0.9817	0.9549	0.9406	0.9006	0.8029	0.6482	0.5132	0.4386	0.2108	0.0429
	14										1.0000	0.9999	0.9997	0.9990	0.9967	0.9902	0.9863	0.9739	0.9365	0.8593	0.7728	0.7161	0.4853	0.1892
	15											1.0000	1.0000	0.9999	0.9997	0.9990	0.9985	0.9967	0.9900	0.9719	0.9459	0.9257	0.8147	0.5599
	16													1.0000	1.0000	1.0000	1.0000	1.0000	1.0000	1.0000	1.0000	1.0000	1.0000	1.0000

The binomial distribution: cumulative probabilities

n	x	0.050	0.100	0.150	$\frac{1}{6}$	0.200	0.250	0.300	$\frac{1}{3}$	0.350	0.400	0.450	0.500	0.550	0.600	0.650	$\frac{2}{3}$	0.700	0.750	0.800	$\frac{5}{6}$	0.850	0.900	0.950
17	0	0.4181	0.1668	0.0631	0.0451	0.0225	0.0075	0.0023	0.0010	0.0007	0.0002	0.0000	0.0000											
	1	0.7922	0.4818	0.2525	0.1983	0.1182	0.0501	0.0193	0.0096	0.0067	0.0021	0.0006	0.0001	0.0000	0.0000									
	2	0.9497	0.7618	0.5198	0.4435	0.3096	0.1637	0.0774	0.0442	0.0327	0.0123	0.0041	0.0012	0.0003	0.0001	0.0000								
	3	0.9912	0.9174	0.7556	0.6887	0.5489	0.3530	0.2019	0.1304	0.1028	0.0464	0.0184	0.0064	0.0019	0.0005	0.0001	0.0000	0.0000						
	4	0.9988	0.9779	0.9013	0.8604	0.7582	0.5739	0.3887	0.2814	0.2348	0.1260	0.0596	0.0245	0.0086	0.0025	0.0006	0.0003	0.0001	0.0000					
	5	0.9999	0.9953	0.9681	0.9496	0.8943	0.7653	0.5968	0.4777	0.4197	0.2639	0.1471	0.0717	0.0301	0.0106	0.0030	0.0019	0.0007	0.0001	0.0000				
	6	1.0000	0.9992	0.9917	0.9853	0.9623	0.8929	0.7752	0.6739	0.6188	0.4478	0.2902	0.1662	0.0826	0.0348	0.0120	0.0080	0.0032	0.0006	0.0001	0.0000			
	7		0.9999	0.9983	0.9965	0.9891	0.9598	0.8954	0.8281	0.7872	0.6405	0.4743	0.3145	0.1834	0.0919	0.0383	0.0273	0.0127	0.0031	0.0005	0.0001	0.0000		
	8		1.0000	0.9997	0.9993	0.9974	0.9876	0.9597	0.9245	0.9006	0.8011	0.6626	0.5000	0.3374	0.1989	0.0994	0.0755	0.0403	0.0124	0.0026	0.0007	0.0003	0.0000	
	9			1.0000	0.9999	0.9995	0.9969	0.9873	0.9727	0.9617	0.9081	0.8166	0.6855	0.5257	0.3595	0.2128	0.1719	0.1046	0.0402	0.0109	0.0035	0.0017	0.0001	
	10				1.0000	0.9999	0.9994	0.9968	0.9920	0.9880	0.9652	0.9174	0.8338	0.7098	0.5522	0.3812	0.3261	0.2248	0.1071	0.0377	0.0147	0.0083	0.0008	0.0000
	11					1.0000	0.9999	0.9993	0.9981	0.9970	0.9894	0.9699	0.9283	0.8529	0.7361	0.5803	0.5223	0.4032	0.2347	0.1057	0.0504	0.0319	0.0047	0.0001
	12						1.0000	0.9999	0.9997	0.9994	0.9975	0.9914	0.9755	0.9404	0.8740	0.7652	0.7186	0.6113	0.4261	0.2418	0.1396	0.0987	0.0221	0.0012
	13							1.0000	1.0000	0.9999	0.9995	0.9981	0.9936	0.9816	0.9536	0.8972	0.8696	0.7981	0.6470	0.4511	0.3113	0.2444	0.0826	0.0088
	14									1.0000	0.9999	0.9997	0.9988	0.9959	0.9877	0.9673	0.9558	0.9226	0.8363	0.6904	0.5565	0.4802	0.2382	0.0503
	15										1.0000	1.0000	0.9999	0.9994	0.9979	0.9933	0.9904	0.9807	0.9499	0.8818	0.8017	0.7475	0.5182	0.2078
	16												1.0000	1.0000	0.9998	0.9993	0.9990	0.9977	0.9925	0.9775	0.9549	0.9369	0.8332	0.5819
	17														1.0000	1.0000	1.0000	1.0000	1.0000	1.0000	1.0000	1.0000	1.0000	1.0000
18	0	0.3972	0.1501	0.0536	0.0376	0.0180	0.0056	0.0016	0.0007	0.0004	0.0001	0.0000	0.0000											
	1	0.7735	0.4503	0.2241	0.1728	0.0991	0.0395	0.0142	0.0068	0.0046	0.0013	0.0003	0.0001	0.0000										
	2	0.9419	0.7338	0.4797	0.4027	0.2713	0.1353	0.0600	0.0326	0.0236	0.0082	0.0025	0.0007	0.0001	0.0000									
	3	0.9891	0.9018	0.7202	0.6479	0.5010	0.3057	0.1646	0.1017	0.0783	0.0328	0.0120	0.0038	0.0010	0.0002	0.0000	0.0000							
	4	0.9985	0.9718	0.8794	0.8318	0.7164	0.5187	0.3327	0.2311	0.1886	0.0942	0.0411	0.0154	0.0049	0.0013	0.0003	0.0002	0.0000						
	5	0.9998	0.9936	0.9581	0.9347	0.8671	0.7175	0.5344	0.4122	0.3550	0.2088	0.1077	0.0481	0.0183	0.0058	0.0014	0.0009	0.0003	0.0000					
	6	1.0000	0.9988	0.9882	0.9794	0.9487	0.8610	0.7217	0.6085	0.5491	0.3743	0.2258	0.1189	0.0537	0.0203	0.0062	0.0039	0.0014	0.0002	0.0000				
	7		0.9998	0.9973	0.9947	0.9837	0.9431	0.8593	0.7767	0.7283	0.5634	0.3915	0.2403	0.1280	0.0576	0.0212	0.0144	0.0061	0.0012	0.0002	0.0000	0.0000		
	8		1.0000	0.9995	0.9989	0.9957	0.9807	0.9404	0.8924	0.8609	0.7368	0.5778	0.4073	0.2527	0.1347	0.0597	0.0433	0.0210	0.0054	0.0009	0.0002	0.0001		
	9			0.9999	0.9998	0.9991	0.9946	0.9790	0.9567	0.9403	0.8653	0.7473	0.5927	0.4222	0.2632	0.1391	0.1076	0.0596	0.0193	0.0043	0.0011	0.0005	0.0000	
	10			1.0000	1.0000	0.9998	0.9988	0.9939	0.9856	0.9788	0.9424	0.8720	0.7597	0.6085	0.4366	0.2717	0.2233	0.1407	0.0569	0.0163	0.0053	0.0027	0.0002	
	11					1.0000	0.9998	0.9986	0.9961	0.9938	0.9797	0.9463	0.8811	0.7742	0.6257	0.4509	0.3915	0.2783	0.1390	0.0513	0.0206	0.0118	0.0012	0.0000
	12						1.0000	0.9997	0.9991	0.9986	0.9942	0.9817	0.9519	0.8923	0.7912	0.6450	0.5878	0.4656	0.2825	0.1329	0.0653	0.0419	0.0064	0.0002
	13							1.0000	0.9998	0.9997	0.9987	0.9951	0.9846	0.9589	0.9058	0.8114	0.7689	0.6673	0.4813	0.2836	0.1682	0.1206	0.0282	0.0015
	14								1.0000	1.0000	0.9998	0.9990	0.9962	0.9880	0.9672	0.9217	0.8983	0.8354	0.6943	0.4990	0.3521	0.2798	0.0982	0.0109
	15										1.0000	0.9999	0.9993	0.9975	0.9918	0.9764	0.9674	0.9400	0.8647	0.7287	0.5973	0.5203	0.2662	0.0581
	16											1.0000	0.9999	0.9997	0.9987	0.9954	0.9932	0.9858	0.9605	0.9009	0.8272	0.7759	0.5497	0.2265
	17												1.0000	1.0000	0.9999	0.9996	0.9993	0.9984	0.9944	0.9820	0.9624	0.9464	0.8499	0.6028
	18														1.0000	1.0000	1.0000	1.0000	1.0000	1.0000	1.0000	1.0000	1.0000	1.0000

The binomial distribution: cumulative probabilities

n	x	0.050	0.100	0.150	$\frac{1}{6}$	0.200	0.250	0.300	$\frac{1}{3}$	0.350	0.400	0.450	0.500	0.550	0.600	0.650	$\frac{2}{3}$	0.700	0.750	0.800	$\frac{5}{6}$	0.850	0.900	0.950
19	0	0.3774	0.1351	0.0456	0.0313	0.0144	0.0042	0.0011	0.0005	0.0003	0.0001	0.0000												
	1	0.7547	0.4203	0.1985	0.1502	0.0829	0.0310	0.0104	0.0047	0.0031	0.0008	0.0002	0.0000											
	2	0.9335	0.7054	0.4413	0.3643	0.2369	0.1113	0.0462	0.0240	0.0170	0.0055	0.0015	0.0004	0.0001	0.0000									
	3	0.9868	0.8850	0.6841	0.6070	0.4551	0.2631	0.1332	0.0787	0.0591	0.0230	0.0077	0.0022	0.0005	0.0001	0.0000	0.0000							
	4	0.9980	0.9648	0.8556	0.8011	0.6733	0.4654	0.2822	0.1879	0.1500	0.0696	0.0280	0.0096	0.0028	0.0006	0.0001	0.0001	0.0000						
	5	0.9998	0.9914	0.9463	0.9176	0.8369	0.6678	0.4739	0.3519	0.2968	0.1629	0.0777	0.0318	0.0109	0.0031	0.0007	0.0004	0.0001	0.0000					
	6	1.0000	0.9983	0.9837	0.9719	0.9324	0.8251	0.6655	0.5431	0.4812	0.3081	0.1727	0.0835	0.0342	0.0116	0.0031	0.0019	0.0006	0.0001					
	7		0.9997	0.9959	0.9921	0.9767	0.9225	0.8180	0.7207	0.6656	0.4878	0.3169	0.1796	0.0871	0.0352	0.0114	0.0074	0.0028	0.0005	0.0000	0.0000			
	8		1.0000	0.9992	0.9982	0.9933	0.9713	0.9161	0.8538	0.8145	0.6675	0.4940	0.3238	0.1841	0.0885	0.0347	0.0241	0.0105	0.0023	0.0003	0.0001	0.0000		
	9			0.9999	0.9996	0.9984	0.9911	0.9674	0.9352	0.9125	0.8139	0.6710	0.5000	0.3290	0.1861	0.0875	0.0648	0.0326	0.0089	0.0016	0.0004	0.0001		
	10			1.0000	0.9999	0.9997	0.9977	0.9895	0.9759	0.9653	0.9115	0.8159	0.6762	0.5060	0.3325	0.1855	0.1462	0.0839	0.0287	0.0067	0.0018	0.0008	0.0000	
	11				1.0000	1.0000	0.9995	0.9972	0.9926	0.9886	0.9648	0.9129	0.8204	0.6831	0.5122	0.3344	0.2793	0.1820	0.0775	0.0233	0.0079	0.0041	0.0003	
	12						0.9999	0.9994	0.9981	0.9969	0.9884	0.9658	0.9165	0.8273	0.6919	0.5188	0.4569	0.3345	0.1749	0.0676	0.0281	0.0163	0.0017	0.0000
	13						1.0000	0.9999	0.9996	0.9993	0.9969	0.9891	0.9682	0.9223	0.8371	0.7032	0.6481	0.5261	0.3322	0.1631	0.0824	0.0537	0.0086	0.0002
	14							1.0000	0.9999	0.9999	0.9994	0.9972	0.9904	0.9720	0.9304	0.8500	0.8121	0.7178	0.5346	0.3267	0.1989	0.1444	0.0352	0.0020
	15								1.0000	1.0000	0.9999	0.9995	0.9978	0.9923	0.9770	0.9409	0.9213	0.8668	0.7369	0.5449	0.3930	0.3159	0.1150	0.0132
	16										1.0000	0.9999	0.9996	0.9985	0.9945	0.9830	0.9760	0.9538	0.8887	0.7631	0.6357	0.5587	0.2946	0.0665
	17											1.0000	1.0000	0.9998	0.9992	0.9969	0.9953	0.9896	0.9690	0.9171	0.8497	0.8015	0.5797	0.2453
	18													1.0000	0.9999	0.9997	0.9995	0.9989	0.9958	0.9856	0.9687	0.9544	0.8649	0.6226
	19														1.0000	1.0000	1.0000	1.0000	1.0000	1.0000	1.0000	1.0000	1.0000	1.0000
20	0	0.3585	0.1216	0.0388	0.0261	0.0115	0.0032	0.0008	0.0003	0.0002	0.0000	0.0000												
	1	0.7358	0.3917	0.1756	0.1304	0.0692	0.0243	0.0076	0.0033	0.0021	0.0005	0.0001	0.0000											
	2	0.9245	0.6769	0.4049	0.3287	0.2061	0.0913	0.0355	0.0176	0.0121	0.0036	0.0009	0.0002	0.0000										
	3	0.9841	0.8670	0.6477	0.5665	0.4114	0.2252	0.1071	0.0604	0.0444	0.0160	0.0049	0.0013	0.0003	0.0000									
	4	0.9974	0.9568	0.8298	0.7687	0.6296	0.4148	0.2375	0.1515	0.1182	0.0510	0.0189	0.0059	0.0015	0.0003	0.0000	0.0000							
	5	0.9997	0.9887	0.9327	0.8982	0.8042	0.6172	0.4164	0.2972	0.2454	0.1256	0.0553	0.0207	0.0064	0.0016	0.0003	0.0002	0.0000						
	6	1.0000	0.9976	0.9781	0.9629	0.9133	0.7858	0.6080	0.4793	0.4166	0.2500	0.1299	0.0577	0.0214	0.0065	0.0015	0.0009	0.0003	0.0000					
	7		0.9996	0.9941	0.9887	0.9679	0.8982	0.7723	0.6615	0.6010	0.4159	0.2520	0.1316	0.0580	0.0210	0.0060	0.0037	0.0013	0.0002	0.0000				
	8		0.9999	0.9987	0.9972	0.9900	0.9591	0.8867	0.8095	0.7624	0.5956	0.4143	0.2517	0.1308	0.0565	0.0196	0.0130	0.0051	0.0009	0.0001	0.0000			
	9		1.0000	0.9998	0.9994	0.9974	0.9861	0.9520	0.9081	0.8782	0.7553	0.5914	0.4119	0.2493	0.1275	0.0532	0.0376	0.0171	0.0039	0.0006	0.0001	0.0000		
	10			1.0000	0.9999	0.9994	0.9961	0.9829	0.9624	0.9468	0.8725	0.7507	0.5881	0.4086	0.2447	0.1218	0.0919	0.0480	0.0139	0.0026	0.0006	0.0002	0.0000	
	11				1.0000	0.9999	0.9991	0.9949	0.9870	0.9804	0.9435	0.8692	0.7483	0.5857	0.4044	0.2376	0.1905	0.1133	0.0409	0.0100	0.0028	0.0013	0.0001	
	12					1.0000	0.9998	0.9987	0.9963	0.9940	0.9790	0.9420	0.8684	0.7480	0.5841	0.3990	0.3385	0.2277	0.1018	0.0321	0.0113	0.0059	0.0004	
	13						1.0000	0.9997	0.9991	0.9985	0.9935	0.9786	0.9423	0.8701	0.7500	0.5834	0.5207	0.3920	0.2142	0.0867	0.0371	0.0219	0.0024	0.0000
	14							1.0000	0.9998	0.9997	0.9984	0.9936	0.9793	0.9447	0.8744	0.7546	0.7028	0.5836	0.3828	0.1958	0.1018	0.0673	0.0113	0.0003
	15								1.0000	1.0000	0.9997	0.9985	0.9941	0.9811	0.9490	0.8818	0.8485	0.7625	0.5852	0.3704	0.2313	0.1702	0.0432	0.0026
	16										1.0000	0.9997	0.9987	0.9951	0.9840	0.9556	0.9396	0.8929	0.7748	0.5886	0.4335	0.3523	0.1330	0.0159
	17											1.0000	0.9998	0.9991	0.9964	0.9879	0.9824	0.9645	0.9087	0.7939	0.6713	0.5951	0.3231	0.0755
	18												1.0000	0.9999	0.9995	0.9979	0.9967	0.9924	0.9757	0.9308	0.8696	0.8244	0.6083	0.2642
	19													1.0000	1.0000	0.9998	0.9997	0.9992	0.9968	0.9885	0.9739	0.9612	0.8784	0.6415
	20															1.0000	1.0000	1.0000	1.0000	1.0000	1.0000	1.0000	1.0000	1.0000

The Poisson distribution: cumulative probabilities

$$P(X \leq x) = \sum_{r=0}^{x} e^{-\lambda}\frac{\lambda^r}{r!}$$

x \ λ	0.01	0.02	0.03	0.04	0.05	0.06	0.07	0.08	0.09
0	0.9900	0.9802	0.9704	0.9608	0.9512	0.9418	0.9324	0.9231	0.9139
1	1.0000	0.9998	0.9996	0.9992	0.9988	0.9983	0.9977	0.9970	0.9962
2		1.0000	1.0000	1.0000	1.0000	1.0000	0.9999	0.9999	0.9999
3							1.0000	1.0000	1.0000

x \ λ	0.10	0.20	0.30	0.40	0.50	0.60	0.70	0.80	0.90
0	0.9048	0.8187	0.7408	0.6703	0.6065	0.5488	0.4966	0.4493	0.4066
1	0.9953	0.9825	0.9631	0.9384	0.9098	0.8781	0.8442	0.8088	0.7725
2	0.9998	0.9989	0.9964	0.9921	0.9856	0.9769	0.9659	0.9526	0.9371
3	1.0000	0.9999	0.9997	0.9992	0.9982	0.9966	0.9942	0.9909	0.9865
4		1.0000	1.0000	0.9999	0.9998	0.9996	0.9992	0.9986	0.9977
5				1.0000	1.0000	1.0000	0.9999	0.9998	0.9997
6							1.0000	1.0000	1.0000

x \ λ	1.00	1.10	1.20	1.30	1.40	1.50	1.60	1.70	1.80	1.90
0	0.3679	0.3329	0.3012	0.2725	0.2466	0.2231	0.2019	0.1827	0.1653	0.1496
1	0.7358	0.6990	0.6626	0.6268	0.5918	0.5578	0.5249	0.4932	0.4628	0.4337
2	0.9197	0.9004	0.8795	0.8571	0.8335	0.8088	0.7834	0.7572	0.7306	0.7037
3	0.9810	0.9743	0.9662	0.9569	0.9463	0.9344	0.9212	0.9068	0.8913	0.8747
4	0.9963	0.9946	0.9923	0.9893	0.9857	0.9814	0.9763	0.9704	0.9636	0.9559
5	0.9994	0.9990	0.9985	0.9978	0.9968	0.9955	0.9940	0.9920	0.9896	0.9868
6	0.9999	0.9999	0.9997	0.9996	0.9994	0.9991	0.9987	0.9981	0.9974	0.9966
7	1.0000	1.0000	1.0000	0.9999	0.9999	0.9998	0.9997	0.9996	0.9994	0.9992
8				1.0000	1.0000	1.0000	0.9999	0.9999	0.9999	0.9998
9							1.0000	1.0000	1.0000	1.0000

x \ λ	2.00	2.10	2.20	2.30	2.40	2.50	2.60	2.70	2.80	2.90
0	0.1353	0.1225	0.1108	0.1003	0.0907	0.0821	0.0743	0.0672	0.0608	0.0550
1	0.4060	0.3796	0.3546	0.3309	0.3084	0.2873	0.2674	0.2487	0.2311	0.2146
2	0.6767	0.6496	0.6227	0.5960	0.5697	0.5438	0.5184	0.4936	0.4695	0.4460
3	0.8571	0.8386	0.8194	0.7993	0.7787	0.7576	0.7360	0.7141	0.6919	0.6696
4	0.9473	0.9379	0.9275	0.9162	0.9041	0.8912	0.8774	0.8629	0.8477	0.8318
5	0.9834	0.9796	0.9751	0.9700	0.9643	0.9580	0.9510	0.9433	0.9349	0.9258
6	0.9955	0.9941	0.9925	0.9906	0.9884	0.9858	0.9828	0.9794	0.9756	0.9713
7	0.9989	0.9985	0.9980	0.9974	0.9967	0.9958	0.9947	0.9934	0.9919	0.9901
8	0.9998	0.9997	0.9995	0.9994	0.9991	0.9989	0.9985	0.9981	0.9976	0.9969
9	1.0000	0.9999	0.9999	0.9999	0.9998	0.9997	0.9996	0.9995	0.9993	0.9991
10		1.0000	1.0000	1.0000	1.0000	0.9999	0.9999	0.9999	0.9998	0.9998
11						1.0000	1.0000	1.0000	1.0000	0.9999

x \ λ	3.00	3.10	3.20	3.30	3.40	3.50	3.60	3.70	3.80	3.90
0	0.0498	0.0450	0.0408	0.0369	0.0334	0.0302	0.0273	0.0247	0.0224	0.0202
1	0.1991	0.1847	0.1712	0.1586	0.1468	0.1359	0.1257	0.1162	0.1074	0.0992
2	0.4232	0.4012	0.3799	0.3594	0.3397	0.3208	0.3027	0.2854	0.2689	0.2531
3	0.6472	0.6248	0.6025	0.5803	0.5584	0.5366	0.5152	0.4942	0.4735	0.4532
4	0.8153	0.7982	0.7806	0.7626	0.7442	0.7254	0.7064	0.6872	0.6678	0.6484
5	0.9161	0.9057	0.8946	0.8829	0.8705	0.8576	0.8441	0.8301	0.8156	0.8006
6	0.9665	0.9612	0.9554	0.9490	0.9421	0.9347	0.9267	0.9182	0.9091	0.8995
7	0.9881	0.9858	0.9832	0.9802	0.9769	0.9733	0.9692	0.9648	0.9599	0.9546
8	0.9962	0.9953	0.9943	0.9931	0.9917	0.9901	0.9883	0.9863	0.9840	0.9815
9	0.9989	0.9986	0.9982	0.9978	0.9973	0.9967	0.9960	0.9952	0.9942	0.9931
10	0.9997	0.9996	0.9995	0.9994	0.9992	0.9990	0.9987	0.9984	0.9981	0.9977
11	0.9999	0.9999	0.9999	0.9998	0.9998	0.9997	0.9996	0.9995	0.9994	0.9993
12	1.0000	1.0000	1.0000	1.0000	1.0000	0.9999	0.9999	0.9999	0.9998	0.9998
13						1.0000	1.0000	1.0000	1.0000	0.9999
14										1.0000

x \ λ	4.00	4.10	4.20	4.30	4.40	4.50	4.60	4.70	4.80	4.90
0	0.0183	0.0166	0.0150	0.0136	0.0123	0.0111	0.0101	0.0091	0.0082	0.0074
1	0.0916	0.0845	0.0780	0.0719	0.0663	0.0611	0.0563	0.0518	0.0477	0.0439
2	0.2381	0.2238	0.2102	0.1974	0.1851	0.1736	0.1626	0.1523	0.1425	0.1333
3	0.4335	0.4142	0.3954	0.3772	0.3594	0.3423	0.3257	0.3097	0.2942	0.2793
4	0.6288	0.6093	0.5898	0.5704	0.5512	0.5321	0.5132	0.4946	0.4763	0.4582
5	0.7851	0.7693	0.7531	0.7367	0.7199	0.7029	0.6858	0.6684	0.6510	0.6335
6	0.8893	0.8786	0.8675	0.8558	0.8436	0.8311	0.8180	0.8046	0.7908	0.7767
7	0.9489	0.9427	0.9361	0.9290	0.9214	0.9134	0.9049	0.8960	0.8867	0.8769
8	0.9786	0.9755	0.9721	0.9683	0.9642	0.9597	0.9549	0.9497	0.9442	0.9382
9	0.9919	0.9905	0.9889	0.9871	0.9851	0.9829	0.9805	0.9778	0.9749	0.9717
10	0.9972	0.9966	0.9959	0.9952	0.9943	0.9933	0.9922	0.9910	0.9896	0.9880
11	0.9991	0.9989	0.9986	0.9983	0.9980	0.9976	0.9971	0.9966	0.9960	0.9953
12	0.9997	0.9997	0.9996	0.9995	0.9993	0.9992	0.9990	0.9988	0.9986	0.9983
13	0.9999	0.9999	0.9999	0.9998	0.9998	0.9997	0.9997	0.9996	0.9995	0.9994
14	1.0000	1.0000	1.0000	1.0000	0.9999	0.9999	0.9999	0.9999	0.9999	0.9998
15					1.0000	1.0000	1.0000	1.0000	1.0000	0.9999
16										1.0000

The Poisson distribution: cumulative probabilities

x \ λ	7.00	7.10	7.20	7.30	7.40	7.50	7.60	7.70	7.80	7.90
0	0.0009	0.0008	0.0007	0.0007	0006	0.0006	0.0005	0.0005	0.0004	0.0004
1	0.0073	0.0067	0.0061	0.0056	0.0051	0.0047	0.0043	0.0039	0.0036	0.0033
2	0.0296	0.0275	0.0255	0.0236	0.0219	0.0203	0.0188	0.0174	0.0161	0.0149
3	0.0818	0.0767	0.0719	0.0674	0.0632	0.0591	0.0554	0.0518	0.0485	0.0453
4	0.1730	0.1641	0.1555	0.1473	0.1395	0.1321	0.1249	0.1181	0.1117	0.1055
5	0.3007	0.2881	0.2759	0.2640	0.2526	0.2414	0.2307	0.2203	0.2103	0.2006
6	0.4497	0.4349	0.4204	0.4060	0.3920	0.3782	0.3646	0.3514	0.3384	0.3257
7	0.5987	0.5838	0.5689	0.5541	0.5393	0.5246	0.5100	0.4956	0.4812	0.4670
8	0.7291	0.7160	0.7027	0.6892	0.6757	0.6620	0.6482	0.6343	0.6204	0.6065
9	0.8305	0.8202	0.8096	0.7988	0.7877	0.7764	0.7649	0.7531	0.7411	0.7290
10	0.9015	0.8942	0.8867	0.8788	0.8707	0.8622	0.8535	0.8445	0.8352	0.8257
11	0.9467	0.9420	0.9371	0.9319	0.9265	0.9208	0.9148	0.9085	0.9020	0.8952
12	0.9730	0.9703	0.9673	0.9642	0.9609	0.9573	0.9536	0.9496	0.9454	0.9409
13	0.9872	0.9857	0.9841	0.9824	0.9805	0.9784	0.9762	0.9739	0.9714	0.9687
14	0.9943	0.9935	0.9927	0.9918	0.9908	0.9897	0.9886	0.9873	0.9859	0.9844
15	0.9976	0.9972	0.9969	0.9964	0.9959	0.9954	0.9948	0.9941	0.9934	0.9926
16	0.9990	0.9989	0.9987	0.9985	0.9983	0.9980	0.9978	0.9974	0.9971	0.9967
17	0.9996	0.9996	0.9995	0.9994	0.9993	0.9992	0.9991	0.9989	0.9988	0.9986
18	0.9999	0.9998	0.9998	0.9998	0.9997	0.9997	0.9996	0.9996	0.9995	0.9994
19	1.0000	0.9999	0.9999	0.9999	0.9999	0.9999	0.9999	0.9998	0.9998	0.9998
20		1.0000	1.0000	1.0000	1.0000	1.0000	1.0000	0.9999	0.9999	0.9999
21								1.0000	1.0000	1.0000

x \ λ	8.00	8.10	8.20	8.30	8.40	8.50	8.60	8.70	8.80	8.90
0	0.0003	0.0003	0.0003	0.0002	0.0002	0.0002	0.0002	0.0002	0.0002	0.0001
1	0.0030	0.0028	0.0025	0.0023	0.0021	0.0019	0.0018	0.0016	0.0015	0.0014
2	0.0138	0.0127	0.0118	0.0109	0.0100	0.0093	0.0086	0.0079	0.0073	0.0068
3	0.0424	0.0396	0.0370	0.0346	0.0323	0.0301	0.0281	0.0262	0.0244	0.0228
4	0.0996	0.0940	0.0887	0.0837	0.0789	0.0744	0.0701	0.0660	0.0621	0.0584
5	0.1912	0.1822	0.1736	0.1653	0.1573	0.1496	0.1422	0.1352	0.1284	0.1219
6	0.3134	0.3013	0.2896	0.2781	0.2670	0.2562	0.2457	0.2355	0.2256	0.2160
7	0.4530	0.4391	0.4254	0.4119	0.3987	0.3856	0.3728	0.3602	0.3478	0.3357
8	0.5925	0.5786	0.5647	0.5507	0.5369	0.5231	0.5094	0.4958	0.4823	0.4689
9	0.7166	0.7041	0.6915	0.6788	0.6659	0.6530	0.6400	0.6269	0.6137	0.6006
10	0.8159	0.8058	0.7955	0.7850	0.7743	0.7634	0.7522	0.7409	0.7294	0.7178
11	0.8881	0.8807	0.8731	0.8652	0.8571	0.8487	0.8400	0.8311	0.8220	0.8126
12	0.9362	0.9313	0.9261	0.9207	0.9150	0.9091	0.9029	0.8965	0.8898	0.8829
13	0.9658	0.9628	0.9595	0.9561	0.9524	0.9486	0.9445	0.9403	0.9358	0.9311
14	0.9827	0.9810	0.9791	0.9771	0.9749	0.9726	0.9701	0.9675	0.9647	0.9617
15	0.9918	0.9908	0.9898	0.9887	0.9875	0.9862	0.9848	0.9832	0.9816	0.9798
16	0.9963	0.9958	0.9953	0.9947	0.9941	0.9934	0.9926	0.9918	0.9909	0.9899
17	0.9984	0.9982	0.9979	0.9977	0.9973	0.9970	0.9966	0.9962	0.9957	0.9952
18	0.9993	0.9992	0.9991	0.9990	0.9989	0.9987	0.9985	0.9983	0.9981	0.9978
19	0.9997	0.9997	0.9997	0.9996	0.9995	0.9995	0.9994	0.9993	0.9992	0.9991
20	0.9999	0.9999	0.9999	0.9998	0.9998	0.9998	0.9998	0.9997	0.9997	0.9996
21	1.0000	1.0000	1.0000	0.9999	0.9999	0.9999	0.9999	0.9999	0.9999	0.9998
22				1.0000	1.0000	1.0000	1.0000	1.0000	1.0000	0.9999
23										1.0000

x \ λ	5.00	5.10	5.20	5.30	5.40	5.50	5.60	5.70	5.80	5.90
0	0.0067	0.0061	0.0055	0.0050	0.0045	0.0041	0.0037	0.0033	0.0030	0.0027
1	0.0404	0.0372	0.0342	0.0314	0.0289	0.0266	0.0244	0.0224	0.0206	0.0189
2	0.1247	0.1165	0.1088	0.1016	0.0948	0.0884	0.0824	0.0768	0.0715	0.0666
3	0.2650	0.2513	0.2381	0.2254	0.2133	0.2017	0.1906	0.1800	0.1700	0.1604
4	0.4405	0.4231	0.4061	0.3895	0.3733	0.3575	0.3422	0.3272	0.3127	0.2987
5	0.6160	0.5984	0.5809	0.5635	0.5461	0.5289	0.5119	0.4950	0.4783	0.4619
6	0.7622	0.7474	0.7324	0.7171	0.7017	0.6860	0.6703	0.6544	0.6384	0.6224
7	0.8666	0.8560	0.8449	0.8335	0.8217	0.8095	0.7970	0.7841	0.7710	0.7576
8	0.9319	0.9252	0.9181	0.9106	0.9027	0.8944	0.8857	0.8766	0.8672	0.8574
9	0.9682	0.9644	0.9603	0.9559	0.9512	0.9462	0.9409	0.9352	0.9292	0.9228
10	0.9863	0.9844	0.9823	0.9800	0.9775	0.9747	0.9718	0.9686	0.9651	0.9614
11	0.9945	0.9937	0.9927	0.9916	0.9904	0.9890	0.9875	0.9859	0.9841	0.9821
12	0.9980	0.9976	0.9972	0.9967	0.9962	0.9955	0.9949	0.9941	0.9932	0.9922
13	0.9993	0.9992	0.9990	0.9988	0.9986	0.9983	0.9980	0.9977	0.9973	0.9969
14	0.9998	0.9997	0.9997	0.9996	0.9995	0.9994	0.9993	0.9991	0.9990	0.9988
15	0.9999	0.9999	0.9999	0.9999	0.9998	0.9998	0.9998	0.9997	0.9996	0.9996
16	1.0000	0.9999	0.9999	0.9999	0.9999	0.9999	0.9999	0.9999	0.9999	0.9999
17		1.0000	1.0000	1.0000	1.0000	1.0000	1.0000	1.0000	1.0000	1.0000

x \ λ	6.00	6.10	6.20	6.30	6.40	6.50	6.60	6.70	6.80	6.90
0	0.0025	0.0022	0.0020	0.0018	0.0017	0.0015	0.0014	0.0012	0.0011	0.0010
1	0.0174	0.0159	0.0146	0.0134	0.0123	0.0113	0.0103	0.0095	0.0087	0.0080
2	0.0620	0.0577	0.0536	0.0498	0.0463	0.0430	0.0400	0.0371	0.0344	0.0320
3	0.1512	0.1425	0.1342	0.1264	0.1189	0.1118	0.1052	0.0988	0.0928	0.0871
4	0.2851	0.2719	0.2592	0.2469	0.2351	0.2237	0.2127	0.2022	0.1920	0.1823
5	0.4457	0.4298	0.4141	0.3988	0.3837	0.3690	0.3547	0.3406	0.3270	0.3137
6	0.6063	0.5902	0.5742	0.5582	0.5423	0.5265	0.5108	0.4953	0.4799	0.4647
7	0.7440	0.7301	0.7160	0.7017	0.6873	0.6728	0.6581	0.6433	0.6285	0.6136
8	0.8472	0.8367	0.8259	0.8148	0.8033	0.7916	0.7796	0.7673	0.7548	0.7420
9	0.9161	0.9090	0.9016	0.8939	0.8858	0.8774	0.8686	0.8596	0.8502	0.8405
10	0.9574	0.9531	0.9486	0.9437	0.9386	0.9332	0.9274	0.9214	0.9151	0.9084
11	0.9799	0.9776	0.9750	0.9723	0.9693	0.9661	0.9627	0.9591	0.9552	0.9510
12	0.9912	0.9900	0.9887	0.9873	0.9857	0.9840	0.9821	0.9801	0.9779	0.9755
13	0.9964	0.9958	0.9952	0.9945	0.9937	0.9929	0.9920	0.9909	0.9898	0.9885
14	0.9986	0.9984	0.9981	0.9978	0.9974	0.9970	0.9966	0.9961	0.9956	0.9950
15	0.9995	0.9994	0.9993	0.9992	0.9990	0.9988	0.9986	0.9984	0.9982	0.9979
16	0.9998	0.9998	0.9997	0.9997	0.9996	0.9996	0.9995	0.9994	0.9993	0.9992
17	0.9999	0.9999	0.9999	0.9999	0.9999	0.9998	0.9998	0.9998	0.9997	0.9997
18	1.0000	1.0000	1.0000	0.9999	0.9999	0.9999	0.9999	0.9999	0.9999	0.9999
19				1.0000	1.0000	1.0000	1.0000	1.0000	1.0000	1.0000

The Poisson distribution: cumulative probabilities

x \ λ	9.00	9.10	9.20	9.30	9.40	9.50	9.60	9.70	9.80	9.90
0	0.0001	0.0001	0.0001	0.0001	0.0001	0.0001	0.0001	0.0001	0.0001	0.0001
1	0.0012	0.0011	0.0010	0.0009	0.0009	0.0008	0.0007	0.0007	0.0006	0.0005
2	0.0062	0.0058	0.0053	0.0049	0.0045	0.0042	0.0038	0.0035	0.0033	0.0030
3	0.0212	0.0198	0.0184	0.0172	0.0160	0.0149	0.0138	0.0129	0.0120	0.0111
4	0.0550	0.0517	0.0486	0.0456	0.0429	0.0403	0.0378	0.0355	0.0333	0.0312
5	0.1157	0.1098	0.1041	0.0986	0.0935	0.0885	0.0838	0.0793	0.0750	0.0710
6	0.2068	0.1978	0.1892	0.1808	0.1727	0.1649	0.1574	0.1502	0.1433	0.1366
7	0.3239	0.3123	0.3010	0.2900	0.2792	0.2687	0.2584	0.2485	0.2388	0.2294
8	0.4557	0.4426	0.4296	0.4168	0.4042	0.3918	0.3796	0.3676	0.3558	0.3442
9	0.5874	0.5742	0.5611	0.5479	0.5349	0.5218	0.5089	0.4960	0.4832	0.4705
10	0.7060	0.6941	0.6820	0.6699	0.6576	0.6453	0.6329	0.6205	0.6080	0.5955
11	0.8030	0.7932	0.7832	0.7730	0.7626	0.7520	0.7412	0.7303	0.7193	0.7081
12	0.8758	0.8684	0.8607	0.8529	0.8448	0.8364	0.8279	0.8191	0.8101	0.8009
13	0.9261	0.9210	0.9156	0.9100	0.9042	0.8981	0.8919	0.8853	0.8786	0.8716
14	0.9585	0.9552	0.9517	0.9480	0.9441	0.9400	0.9357	0.9312	0.9265	0.9216
15	0.9780	0.9760	0.9738	0.9715	0.9691	0.9665	0.9638	0.9609	0.9579	0.9546
16	0.9889	0.9878	0.9865	0.9852	0.9838	0.9823	0.9806	0.9789	0.9770	0.9751
17	0.9947	0.9941	0.9934	0.9927	0.9919	0.9911	0.9902	0.9892	0.9881	0.9870
18	0.9976	0.9973	0.9969	0.9966	0.9962	0.9957	0.9952	0.9947	0.9941	0.9935
19	0.9989	0.9988	0.9986	0.9985	0.9983	0.9980	0.9978	0.9975	0.9972	0.9969
20	0.9996	0.9995	0.9994	0.9993	0.9992	0.9991	0.9990	0.9989	0.9987	0.9986
21	0.9998	0.9998	0.9998	0.9997	0.9997	0.9996	0.9996	0.9995	0.9995	0.9994
22	0.9999	0.9999	0.9999	0.9999	0.9999	0.9999	0.9998	0.9998	0.9998	0.9997
23	1.0000	0.9999	0.9999	0.9999	0.9999	0.9999	0.9999	0.9999	0.9999	0.9999
24		1.0000	1.0000	1.0000	1.0000	1.0000	1.0000	1.0000	1.0000	1.0000

x \ λ	10.00	10.10	10.20	10.30	10.40	10.50	10.60	10.70	10.80	10.90
0	0.0000	0.0000	0.0000	0.0000	0.0000	0.0000	0.0000	0.0000	0.0000	0.0000
1	0.0005	0.0005	0.0004	0.0004	0.0003	0.0003	0.0003	0.0003	0.0002	0.0002
2	0.0028	0.0026	0.0023	0.0022	0.0020	0.0018	0.0017	0.0016	0.0014	0.0013
3	0.0103	0.0096	0.0089	0.0083	0.0077	0.0071	0.0066	0.0062	0.0057	0.0053
4	0.0293	0.0274	0.0257	0.0241	0.0225	0.0211	0.0197	0.0185	0.0173	0.0162
5	0.0671	0.0634	0.0599	0.0566	0.0534	0.0504	0.0475	0.0448	0.0423	0.0398
6	0.1301	0.1240	0.1180	0.1123	0.1069	0.1016	0.0966	0.0918	0.0872	0.0828
7	0.2202	0.2113	0.2027	0.1944	0.1863	0.1785	0.1710	0.1636	0.1566	0.1498
8	0.3328	0.3217	0.3108	0.3001	0.2896	0.2794	0.2694	0.2597	0.2502	0.2410
9	0.4579	0.4455	0.4332	0.4210	0.4090	0.3971	0.3854	0.3739	0.3626	0.3515
10	0.5830	0.5705	0.5580	0.5456	0.5331	0.5207	0.5084	0.4961	0.4840	0.4719
11	0.6968	0.6853	0.6738	0.6622	0.6505	0.6387	0.6269	0.6150	0.6031	0.5912
12	0.7916	0.7820	0.7722	0.7623	0.7522	0.7420	0.7316	0.7210	0.7104	0.6996
13	0.8645	0.8571	0.8494	0.8416	0.8336	0.8253	0.8169	0.8083	0.7995	0.7905
14	0.9165	0.9112	0.9057	0.9000	0.8940	0.8879	0.8815	0.8750	0.8682	0.8612
15	0.9513	0.9477	0.9440	0.9400	0.9359	0.9317	0.9272	0.9225	0.9177	0.9126
16	0.9730	0.9707	0.9684	0.9658	0.9632	0.9604	0.9574	0.9543	0.9511	0.9477
17	0.9857	0.9844	0.9830	0.9815	0.9799	0.9781	0.9763	0.9744	0.9723	0.9701
18	0.9928	0.9921	0.9913	0.9904	0.9895	0.9885	0.9874	0.9863	0.9850	0.9837
19	0.9965	0.9962	0.9957	0.9953	0.9948	0.9942	0.9936	0.9930	0.9923	0.9915
20	0.9984	0.9982	0.9980	0.9978	0.9975	0.9972	0.9969	0.9966	0.9962	0.9958
21	0.9993	0.9992	0.9991	0.9990	0.9989	0.9987	0.9986	0.9984	0.9982	0.9980
22	0.9997	0.9997	0.9996	0.9996	0.9995	0.9994	0.9994	0.9993	0.9992	0.9991
23	0.9999	0.9999	0.9998	0.9998	0.9998	0.9998	0.9997	0.9997	0.9996	0.9996
24	1.0000	0.9999	0.9999	0.9999	0.9999	0.9999	0.9999	0.9999	0.9998	0.9998
25		1.0000	1.0000	1.0000	1.0000	1.0000	1.0000	1.0000	0.9999	0.9999
26									1.0000	1.0000

Critical values for the product moment correlation coefficient, r

1-tailed	5%	2½%	1%	½%
2-tailed	10%	5%	2%	1%
n				
1				
2				
3	0.9877	0.9969	0.9995	0.9999
4	0.9000	0.9500	0.9800	0.9900
5	0.8054	0.8783	0.9343	0.9587
6	0.7293	0.8114	0.8822	0.9172
7	0.6694	0.7545	0.8329	0.8745
8	0.6215	0.7067	0.7887	0.8343
9	0.5822	0.6664	0.7498	0.7977
10	0.5494	0.6319	0.7155	0.7646
11	0.5214	0.6021	0.6851	0.7348
12	0.4973	0.5760	0.6581	0.7079
13	0.4762	0.5529	0.6339	0.6835
14	0.4575	0.5324	0.6120	0.6614
15	0.4409	0.5140	0.5923	0.6411
16	0.4259	0.4973	0.5742	0.6226
17	0.4124	0.4821	0.5577	0.6055
18	0.4000	0.4683	0.5425	0.5897
19	0.3887	0.4555	0.5285	0.5751
20	0.3783	0.4438	0.5155	0.5614
21	0.3687	0.4329	0.5034	0.5487
22	0.3598	0.4227	0.4921	0.5368
23	0.3515	0.4132	0.4815	0.5256
24	0.3438	0.4044	0.4716	0.5151
25	0.3365	0.3961	0.4622	0.5052
26	0.3297	0.3882	0.4534	0.4958
27	0.3233	0.3809	0.4451	0.4869
28	0.3172	0.3739	0.4372	0.4785
29	0.3115	0.3673	0.4297	0.4705
30	0.3061	0.3610	0.4226	0.4629

1-tailed	5%	2½%	1%	½%
2-tailed	10%	5%	2%	1%
n				
31	0.3009	0.3550	0.4158	0.4556
32	0.2960	0.3494	0.4093	0.4487
33	0.2913	0.3440	0.4032	0.4421
34	0.2869	0.3388	0.3972	0.4357
35	0.2826	0.3338	0.3916	0.4296
36	0.2785	0.3291	0.3862	0.4238
37	0.2746	0.3246	0.3810	0.4182
38	0.2709	0.3202	0.3760	0.4128
39	0.2673	0.3160	0.3712	0.4076
40	0.2638	0.3120	0.3665	0.4026
41	0.2605	0.3081	0.3621	0.3978
42	0.2573	0.3044	0.3578	0.3932
43	0.2542	0.3008	0.3536	0.3887
44	0.2512	0.2973	0.3496	0.3843
45	0.2483	0.2940	0.3457	0.3801
46	0.2455	0.2907	0.3420	0.3761
47	0.2429	0.2876	0.3384	0.3721
48	0.2403	0.2845	0.3348	0.3683
49	0.2377	0.2816	0.3314	0.3646
50	0.2353	0.2787	0.3281	0.3610
51	0.2329	0.2759	0.3249	0.3575
52	0.2306	0.2732	0.3218	0.3542
53	0.2284	0.2706	0.3188	0.3509
54	0.2262	0.2681	0.3158	0.3477
55	0.2241	0.2656	0.3129	0.3445
56	0.2221	0.2632	0.3102	0.3415
57	0.2201	0.2609	0.3074	0.3385
58	0.2181	0.2586	0.3048	0.3357
59	0.2162	0.2564	0.3022	0.3328
60	0.2144	0.2542	0.2997	0.3301

Critical values for Spearman's rank correlation coefficient, r_s

1-tailed	5%	2½%	1%	½%
2-tailed	10%	5%	2%	1%
n				
1				
2				
3				
4	1.0000			
5	0.9000	1.0000	1.0000	
6	0.8286	0.8857	0.9429	1.0000
7	0.7143	0.7857	0.8929	0.9286
8	0.6429	0.7381	0.8333	0.8810
9	0.6000	0.7000	0.7833	0.8333
10	0.5636	0.6485	0.7455	0.7939
11	0.5364	0.6182	0.7091	0.7545
12	0.5035	0.5874	0.6783	0.7273
13	0.4835	0.5604	0.6484	0.7033
14	0.4637	0.5385	0.6264	0.6791
15	0.4464	0.5214	0.6036	0.6536
16	0.4294	0.5029	0.5824	0.6353
17	0.4142	0.4877	0.5662	0.6176
18	0.4014	0.4716	0.5501	0.5996
19	0.3912	0.4596	0.5351	0.5842
20	0.3805	0.4466	0.5218	0.5699
21	0.3701	0.4364	0.5091	0.5558
22	0.3608	0.4252	0.4975	0.5438
23	0.3528	0.4160	0.4862	0.5316
24	0.3443	0.4070	0.4757	0.5209
25	0.3369	0.3977	0.4662	0.5108
26	0.3306	0.3901	0.4571	0.5009
27	0.3242	0.3828	0.4487	0.4915
28	0.3180	0.3755	0.4401	0.4828
29	0.3118	0.3685	0.4325	0.4749
30	0.3063	0.3624	0.4251	0.4670

1-tailed	5%	2½%	1%	½%
2-tailed	10%	5%	2%	1%
n				
31	0.3012	0.3560	0.4185	0.4593
32	0.2962	0.3504	0.4117	0.4523
33	0.2914	0.3449	0.4054	0.4455
34	0.2871	0.3396	0.3995	0.4390
35	0.2829	0.3347	0.3936	0.4328
36	0.2788	0.3300	0.3882	0.4268
37	0.2748	0.3253	0.3829	0.4211
38	0.2710	0.3209	0.3778	0.4155
39	0.2674	0.3168	0.3729	0.4103
40	0.2640	0.3128	0.3681	0.4051
41	0.2606	0.3087	0.3636	0.4002
42	0.2574	0.3051	0.3594	0.3955
43	0.2543	0.3014	0.3550	0.3908
44	0.2513	0.2978	0.3511	0.3865
45	0.2484	0.2945	0.3470	0.3822
46	0.2455	0.2913	0.3433	0.3781
47	0.2429	0.2880	0.3396	0.3741
48	0.2403	0.2850	0.3361	0.3702
49	0.2378	0.2820	0.3326	0.3664
50	0.2353	0.2791	0.3293	0.3628
51	0.2329	0.2764	0.3260	0.3592
52	0.2307	0.2736	0.3228	0.3558
53	0.2284	0.2710	0.3198	0.3524
54	0.2262	0.2685	0.3168	0.3492
55	0.2242	0.2659	0.3139	0.3460
56	0.2221	0.2636	0.3111	0.3429
57	0.2201	0.2612	0.3083	0.3400
58	0.2181	0.2589	0.3057	0.3370
59	0.2162	0.2567	0.3030	0.3342
60	0.2144	0.2545	0.3005	0.3314

The Normal distribution: values of $\Phi(z) = p$

The table gives the probability, p, of a random variable distributed as N(0, 1) being less than z.

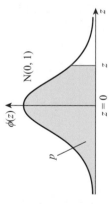

z	.00	.01	.02	.03	.04	.05	.06	.07	.08	.09	1	2	3	4	5	6	7	8	9
0.0	.5000	5040	5080	5120	5160	5199	5239	5279	5319	5359	4	8	12	16	20	24	28	32	36
0.1	.5398	5438	5478	5517	5557	5596	5636	5675	5714	5753	4	8	12	16	20	24	28	32	35
0.2	.5793	5832	5871	5910	5948	5987	6026	6064	6103	6141	4	8	12	15	19	23	27	31	35
0.3	.6179	6217	6255	6293	6331	6368	6406	6443	6480	6517	4	8	11	15	19	23	26	30	34
0.4	.6554	6591	6628	6664	6700	6736	6772	6808	6844	6879	4	7	11	14	18	22	25	29	32
0.5	.6915	6950	6985	7019	7054	7088	7123	7157	7190	7224	3	7	10	14	17	21	24	27	31
0.6	.7257	7291	7324	7357	7389	7422	7454	7486	7517	7549	3	6	10	13	16	19	23	26	29
0.7	.7580	7611	7642	7673	7704	7734	7764	7794	7823	7852	3	6	9	12	15	18	21	24	27
0.8	.7881	7910	7939	7967	7995	8023	8051	8078	8106	8133	3	6	8	11	14	17	19	22	25
0.9	.8159	8186	8212	8238	8264	8289	8315	8340	8365	8389	3	5	8	10	13	15	18	20	23
1.0	.8413	8438	8461	8485	8508	8531	8554	8577	8599	8621	2	5	7	9	12	14	16	18	21
1.1	.8643	8665	8686	8708	8729	8749	8770	8790	8810	8830	2	4	6	8	10	12	14	16	19
1.2	.8849	8869	8888	8907	8925	8944	8962	8980	8997	9015	2	4	6	7	9	11	13	15	16
1.3	.9032	9049	9066	9082	9099	9115	9131	9147	9162	9177	2	3	5	6	8	10	11	13	14
1.4	.9192	9207	9222	9236	9251	9265	9279	9292	9306	9319	1	3	4	6	7	8	10	11	13
1.5	.9332	9345	9357	9370	9382	9394	9406	9418	9429	9441	1	2	4	5	6	7	8	10	11
1.6	.9452	9463	9474	9484	9495	9505	9515	9525	9535	9545	1	2	3	4	5	6	7	8	9
1.7	.9554	9564	9573	9582	9591	9599	9608	9616	9625	9633	1	2	3	4	4	5	6	7	8
1.8	.9641	9649	9656	9664	9671	9678	9686	9693	9699	9706	1	1	2	3	4	4	5	6	6
1.9	.9713	9719	9726	9732	9738	9744	9750	9756	9761	9767	1	1	2	2	3	4	4	5	5
2.0	.9772	9778	9783	9788	9793	9798	9803	9808	9812	9817	0	1	1	2	2	3	3	4	4
2.1	.9821	9826	9830	9834	9838	9842	9846	9850	9854	9857	0	1	1	2	2	2	3	3	4
2.2	.9861	9864	9868	9871	9875	9878	9881	9884	9887	9890	0	1	1	1	2	2	2	3	3
2.3	.9893	9896	9898	9901	9904	9906	9909	9911	9913	9916	0	1	1	1	1	2	2	2	3
2.4	.9918	9920	9922	9925	9927	9929	9931	9932	9934	9936	0	0	1	1	1	1	2	2	2
2.5	.9938	9940	9941	9943	9945	9946	9948	9949	9951	9952									
2.6	.9953	9955	9956	9957	9959	9960	9961	9962	9963	9964									
2.7	.9965	9966	9967	9968	9969	9970	9971	9972	9973	9974									
2.8	.9974	9975	9976	9977	9977	9978	9979	9979	9980	9981					_differences_				
2.9	.9981	9982	9982	9983	9984	9984	9985	9985	9986	9986					_untrustworthy_				
3.0	.9987	9987	9987	9988	9988	9989	9989	9989	9990	9990									
3.1	.9990	9991	9991	9991	9992	9992	9992	9992	9993	9993									
3.2	.9993	9993	9994	9994	9994	9994	9994	9995	9995	9995									
3.3	.9995	9995	9995	9996	9996	9996	9996	9996	9996	9997									
3.4	.9997	9997	9997	9997	9997	9997	9997	9997	9997	9998									

The inverse Normal distribution: values of $\Phi^{-1}(p) = z$

p	.000	.001	.002	.003	.004	.005	.006	.007	.008	.009
.50	.0000	.0025	.0050	.0075	.0100	.0125	.0150	.0175	.0201	.0226
.51	.0251	.0276	.0301	.0326	.0351	.0376	.0401	.0426	.0451	.0476
.52	.0502	.0527	.0552	.0577	.0602	.0627	.0652	.0677	.0702	.0728
.53	.0753	.0778	.0803	.0828	.0853	.0878	.0904	.0929	.0954	.0979
.54	.1004	.1030	.1055	.1080	.1105	.1130	.1156	.1181	.1206	.1231
.55	.1257	.1282	.1307	.1332	.1358	.1383	.1408	.1434	.1459	.1484
.56	.1510	.1535	.1560	.1586	.1611	.1637	.1662	.1687	.1713	.1738
.57	.1764	.1789	.1815	.1840	.1866	.1891	.1917	.1942	.1968	.1993
.58	.2019	.2045	.2070	.2096	.2121	.2147	.2173	.2198	.2224	.2250
.59	.2275	.2301	.2327	.2353	.2378	.2404	.2430	.2456	.2482	.2508
.60	.2533	.2559	.2585	.2611	.2637	.2663	.2689	.2715	.2741	.2767
.61	.2793	.2819	.2845	.2871	.2898	.2924	.2950	.2976	.3002	.3029
.62	.3055	.3081	.3107	.3134	.3160	.3186	.3213	.3239	.3266	.3292
.63	.3319	.3345	.3372	.3398	.3425	.3451	.3478	.3505	.3531	.3558
.64	.3585	.3611	.3638	.3665	.3692	.3719	.3745	.3772	.3799	.3826
.65	.3853	.3880	.3907	.3934	.3961	.3989	.4016	.4043	.4070	.4097
.66	.4125	.4152	.4179	.4207	.4234	.4261	.4289	.4316	.4344	.4372
.67	.4399	.4427	.4454	.4482	.4510	.4538	.4565	.4593	.4621	.4649
.68	.4677	.4705	.4733	.4761	.4789	.4817	.4845	.4874	.4902	.4930
.69	.4959	.4987	.5015	.5044	.5072	.5101	.5129	.5158	.5187	.5215
.70	.5244	.5273	.5302	.5330	.5359	.5388	.5417	.5446	.5476	.5505
.71	.5534	.5563	.5592	.5622	.5651	.5681	.5710	.5740	.5769	.5799
.72	.5828	.5858	.5888	.5918	.5948	.5978	.6008	.6038	.6068	.6098
.73	.6128	.6158	.6189	.6219	.6250	.6280	.6311	.6341	.6372	.6403
.74	.6433	.6464	.6495	.6526	.6557	.6588	.6620	.6651	.6682	.6713
.75	.6745	.6776	.6808	.6840	.6871	.6903	.6935	.6967	.6999	.7031
.76	.7063	.7095	.7128	.7160	.7192	.7225	.7257	.7290	.7323	.7356
.77	.7388	.7421	.7454	.7488	.7521	.7554	.7588	.7621	.7655	.7688
.78	.7722	.7756	.7790	.7824	.7858	.7892	.7926	.7961	.7995	.8030
.79	.8064	.8099	.8134	.8169	.8204	.8239	.8274	.8310	.8345	.8381
.80	.8416	.8452	.8488	.8524	.8560	.8596	.8633	.8669	.8705	.8742
.81	.8779	.8816	.8853	.8890	.8927	.8965	.9002	.9040	.9078	.9116
.82	.9154	.9192	.9230	.9269	.9307	.9346	.9385	.9424	.9463	.9502
.83	.9542	.9581	.9621	.9661	.9701	.9741	.9782	.9822	.9863	.9904
.84	.9945	.9986	1.003	1.007	1.011	1.015	1.019	1.024	1.028	1.032
.85	1.036	1.041	1.045	1.049	1.054	1.058	1.063	1.067	1.071	1.076
.86	1.080	1.085	1.089	1.094	1.099	1.103	1.108	1.112	1.117	1.122
.87	1.126	1.131	1.136	1.141	1.146	1.150	1.155	1.160	1.165	1.170
.88	1.175	1.180	1.185	1.190	1.195	1.200	1.206	1.211	1.216	1.221
.89	1.227	1.232	1.237	1.243	1.248	1.254	1.259	1.265	1.270	1.276
.90	1.282	1.287	1.293	1.299	1.305	1.311	1.317	1.323	1.329	1.335
.91	1.341	1.347	1.353	1.360	1.366	1.372	1.379	1.385	1.392	1.398
.92	1.405	1.412	1.419	1.426	1.433	1.440	1.447	1.454	1.461	1.468
.93	1.476	1.483	1.491	1.499	1.506	1.514	1.522	1.530	1.538	1.546
.94	1.555	1.563	1.572	1.581	1.589	1.598	1.607	1.616	1.626	1.635
.95	1.645	1.655	1.665	1.675	1.685	1.695	1.706	1.717	1.728	1.739
.96	1.751	1.762	1.774	1.787	1.799	1.812	1.825	1.838	1.852	1.866
.97	1.881	1.896	1.911	1.927	1.943	1.960	1.977	1.995	2.014	2.034
.98	2.054	2.075	2.097	2.120	2.144	2.170	2.197	2.226	2.257	2.290
.99	2.326	2.366	2.409	2.457	2.512	2.576	2.652	2.748	2.878	3.090

Percentage points of the *t* distribution

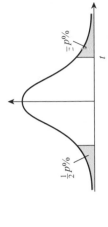

p% / v	10	5	2	1
1	6.314	12.71	31.82	63.66
2	2.920	4.303	6.965	9.925
3	2.353	3.182	4.541	5.841
4	2.132	2.776	3.747	4.604
5	2.015	2.571	3.365	4.032
6	1.943	2.447	3.143	3.707
7	1.895	2.365	2.998	3.499
8	1.860	2.306	2.896	3.355
9	1.833	2.262	2.821	3.250
10	1.812	2.228	2.764	3.169
11	1.796	2.201	2.718	3.106
12	1.782	2.179	2.681	3.055
13	1.771	2.160	2.650	3.012
14	1.761	2.145	2.624	2.977
15	1.753	2.131	2.602	2.947
20	1.725	2.086	2.528	2.845
30	1.697	2.042	2.457	2.750
50	1.676	2.009	2.403	2.678
100	1.660	1.984	2.364	2.626
∞	1.645	1.960	2.326	2.576

∞ = percentage points of the Normal distribution N(0, 1)

Percentage points of the χ^2 (chi-squared) distribution

p% / v	99	97.5	95	90	10	5.0	2.5	1.0	0.5
1	.0001	.0010	.0039	.0158	2.706	3.841	5.024	6.635	7.879
2	.0201	.0506	0.103	0.211	4.605	5.991	7.378	9.210	10.60
3	0.115	0.216	0.352	0.584	6.251	7.815	9.348	11.34	12.84
4	0.297	0.484	0.711	1.064	7.779	9.488	11.14	13.28	14.86
5	0.554	0.831	1.145	1.610	9.236	11.07	12.83	15.09	16.75
6	0.872	1.237	1.635	2.204	10.64	12.59	14.45	16.81	18.55
7	1.239	1.690	2.167	2.833	12.02	14.07	16.01	18.48	20.28
8	1.646	2.180	2.733	3.490	13.36	15.51	17.53	20.09	21.95
9	2.088	2.700	3.325	4.168	14.68	16.92	19.02	21.67	23.59
10	2.558	3.247	3.940	4.865	15.99	18.31	20.48	23.21	25.19
11	3.053	3.816	4.575	5.578	17.28	19.68	21.92	24.72	26.76
12	3.571	4.404	5.226	6.304	18.55	21.03	23.34	26.22	28.30
13	4.107	5.009	5.892	7.042	19.81	22.36	24.74	27.69	29.82
14	4.660	5.629	6.571	7.790	21.06	23.68	26.12	29.14	31.32
15	5.229	6.262	7.261	8.547	22.31	25.00	27.49	30.58	32.80
16	5.812	6.908	7.962	9.312	23.54	26.30	28.85	32.00	34.27
17	6.408	7.564	8.672	10.09	24.77	27.59	30.19	33.41	35.72
18	7.015	8.231	9.390	10.86	25.99	28.87	31.53	34.81	37.16
19	7.633	8.907	10.12	11.65	27.20	30.14	32.85	36.19	38.58
20	8.260	9.591	10.85	12.44	28.41	31.41	34.17	37.57	40.00
21	8.897	10.28	11.59	13.24	29.62	32.67	35.48	38.93	41.40
22	9.542	10.98	12.34	14.04	30.81	33.92	36.78	40.29	42.80
23	10.20	11.69	13.09	14.85	32.01	35.17	38.08	41.64	44.18
24	10.86	12.40	13.85	15.66	33.20	36.42	39.36	42.98	45.56
25	11.52	13.12	14.61	16.47	34.38	37.65	40.65	44.31	46.93
26	12.20	13.84	15.38	17.29	35.56	38.89	41.92	45.64	48.29
27	12.88	14.57	16.15	18.11	36.74	40.11	43.19	46.96	49.64
28	13.56	15.31	16.93	18.94	37.92	41.34	44.46	48.28	50.99
29	14.26	16.05	17.71	19.77	39.09	42.56	45.72	49.59	52.34
30	14.95	16.79	18.49	20.60	40.26	43.77	46.98	50.89	53.67
35	18.51	20.57	22.47	24.80	46.06	49.80	53.20	57.34	60.27
40	22.16	24.43	26.51	29.05	51.81	55.76	59.34	63.69	66.77
50	29.71	32.36	34.76	37.69	63.17	67.50	71.42	76.15	79.49
100	70.06	74.22	77.93	82.36	118.5	124.3	129.6	135.8	140.2

Critical values for the F test

2½% points of the F distribution

v_2 \ v_1	1	2	3	4	5	6	7	8	10	12	24	∞
1	648	800	864	900	922	937	948	957	969	977	997	1018
2	38.5	39.0	39.2	39.2	39.3	39.3	39.4	39.4	39.4	39.4	39.5	39.5
3	17.4	16.0	15.4	15.1	14.9	14.7	14.6	14.5	14.4	14.3	14.1	13.9
4	12.22	10.65	9.98	9.60	9.36	9.20	9.07	8.98	8.84	8.75	8.51	8.26
5	10.01	8.43	7.76	7.39	7.15	6.98	6.85	6.76	6.62	6.52	6.28	6.02
6	8.81	7.26	6.60	6.23	5.99	5.82	5.70	5.60	5.46	5.37	5.12	4.85
7	8.07	6.54	5.89	5.52	5.29	5.12	4.99	4.90	4.76	4.67	4.42	4.14
8	7.57	6.06	5.42	5.05	4.82	4.65	4.53	4.43	4.30	4.20	3.95	3.67
9	7.21	5.71	5.08	4.72	4.48	4.32	4.20	4.10	3.96	3.87	3.61	3.33
10	6.94	5.46	4.83	4.47	4.24	4.07	3.95	3.85	3.72	3.62	3.37	3.08
11	6.72	5.26	4.63	4.28	4.04	3.88	3.76	3.66	3.53	3.43	3.17	2.88
12	6.55	5.10	4.47	4.12	3.89	3.73	3.61	3.51	3.37	3.28	3.02	2.72
13	6.41	4.97	4.35	4.00	3.77	3.60	3.48	3.39	3.25	3.15	2.89	2.60
14	6.30	4.86	4.24	3.89	3.66	3.50	3.38	3.29	3.15	3.05	2.79	2.49
15	6.20	4.76	4.15	3.80	3.58	3.41	3.29	3.20	3.06	2.96	2.70	2.40
16	6.12	4.69	4.08	3.73	3.50	3.34	3.22	3.12	2.99	2.89	2.63	2.32
17	6.04	4.62	4.01	3.66	3.44	3.28	3.16	3.06	2.92	2.82	2.56	2.25
18	5.98	4.56	3.95	3.61	3.38	3.22	3.10	3.01	2.87	2.77	2.50	2.19
19	5.92	4.51	3.90	3.56	3.33	3.17	3.05	2.96	2.82	2.72	2.45	2.13
20	5.87	4.46	3.86	3.51	3.29	3.13	3.01	2.91	2.77	2.68	2.41	2.09
21	5.83	4.42	3.82	3.48	3.25	3.09	2.97	2.87	2.73	2.64	2.37	2.04
22	5.79	4.38	3.78	3.44	3.22	3.05	2.93	2.84	2.70	2.60	2.33	2.00
23	5.75	4.35	3.75	3.41	3.18	3.02	2.90	2.81	2.67	2.57	2.30	1.97
24	5.72	4.32	3.72	3.38	3.15	2.99	2.87	2.78	2.64	2.54	2.27	1.94
25	5.69	4.29	3.69	3.35	3.13	2.97	2.85	2.75	2.61	2.51	2.24	1.91
26	5.66	4.27	3.67	3.33	3.10	2.94	2.82	2.73	2.59	2.49	2.22	1.88
27	5.63	4.24	3.65	3.31	3.08	2.92	2.80	2.71	2.57	2.47	2.19	1.85
28	5.61	4.22	3.63	3.29	3.06	2.90	2.78	2.69	2.55	2.45	2.17	1.83
29	5.59	4.20	3.61	3.27	3.04	2.88	2.76	2.67	2.53	2.43	2.15	1.81
30	5.57	4.18	3.59	3.25	3.03	2.87	2.75	2.65	2.51	2.41	2.14	1.79
32	5.53	4.15	3.56	3.22	3.00	2.84	2.72	2.62	2.48	2.38	2.10	1.75
34	5.50	4.12	3.53	3.19	2.97	2.81	2.69	2.59	2.45	2.35	2.08	1.72
36	5.47	4.09	3.51	3.17	2.94	2.79	2.66	2.57	2.43	2.33	2.05	1.69
38	5.45	4.07	3.48	3.15	2.92	2.76	2.64	2.55	2.41	2.31	2.03	1.66
40	5.42	4.05	3.46	3.13	2.90	2.74	2.62	2.53	2.39	2.29	2.01	1.64
60	5.29	3.93	3.34	3.01	2.79	2.63	2.51	2.41	2.27	2.17	1.88	1.48
120	5.15	3.80	3.23	2.89	2.67	2.52	2.39	2.30	2.16	2.05	1.76	1.31
∞	5.02	3.69	3.12	2.79	2.57	2.41	2.29	2.19	2.05	1.94	1.64	1.00

5% points of the F distribution

v_2 \ v_1	1	2	3	4	5	6	7	8	10	12	24	∞
1	161.4	199.5	215.7	224.6	230.2	234.0	236.8	238.9	241.9	243.9	249.0	254.3
2	18.5	19.0	19.2	19.2	19.3	19.3	19.4	19.4	19.4	19.4	19.5	19.5
3	10.13	9.55	9.28	9.12	9.01	8.94	8.89	8.85	8.79	8.74	8.64	8.53
4	7.71	6.94	6.59	6.39	6.26	6.16	6.09	6.04	5.96	5.91	5.77	5.63
5	6.61	5.79	5.41	5.19	5.05	4.95	4.88	4.82	4.74	4.68	4.53	4.36
6	5.99	5.14	4.76	4.53	4.39	4.28	4.21	4.15	4.06	4.00	3.84	3.67
7	5.59	4.74	4.35	4.12	3.97	3.87	3.79	3.73	3.64	3.57	3.41	3.23
8	5.32	4.46	4.07	3.84	3.69	3.58	3.50	3.44	3.35	3.28	3.12	2.93
9	5.12	4.26	3.86	3.63	3.48	3.37	3.29	3.23	3.14	3.07	2.90	2.71
10	4.96	4.10	3.71	3.48	3.33	3.22	3.14	3.07	2.98	2.91	2.74	2.54
11	4.84	3.98	3.59	3.36	3.20	3.09	3.01	2.95	2.85	2.79	2.61	2.40
12	4.75	3.89	3.49	3.26	3.11	3.00	2.91	2.85	2.75	2.69	2.51	2.30
13	4.67	3.81	3.41	3.18	3.03	2.92	2.83	2.77	2.67	2.60	2.42	2.21
14	4.60	3.74	3.34	3.11	2.96	2.85	2.76	2.70	2.60	2.53	2.35	2.13
15	4.54	3.68	3.29	3.06	2.90	2.79	2.71	2.64	2.54	2.48	2.29	2.07
16	4.49	3.63	3.24	3.01	2.85	2.74	2.66	2.59	2.49	2.42	2.24	2.01
17	4.45	3.59	3.20	2.96	2.81	2.70	2.61	2.55	2.45	2.38	2.19	1.96
18	4.41	3.55	3.16	2.93	2.77	2.66	2.58	2.51	2.41	2.34	2.15	1.92
19	4.38	3.52	3.13	2.90	2.74	2.63	2.54	2.48	2.38	2.31	2.11	1.88
20	4.35	3.49	3.10	2.87	2.71	2.60	2.51	2.45	2.35	2.28	2.08	1.84
21	4.32	3.47	3.07	2.84	2.68	2.57	2.49	2.42	2.32	2.25	2.05	1.81
22	4.30	3.44	3.05	2.82	2.66	2.55	2.46	2.40	2.30	2.23	2.03	1.78
23	4.28	3.42	3.03	2.80	2.64	2.53	2.44	2.37	2.27	2.20	2.00	1.76
24	4.26	3.40	3.01	2.78	2.62	2.51	2.42	2.36	2.25	2.18	1.98	1.73
25	4.24	3.39	2.99	2.76	2.60	2.49	2.40	2.34	2.24	2.16	1.96	1.71
26	4.23	3.37	2.98	2.74	2.59	2.47	2.39	2.32	2.22	2.15	1.95	1.69
27	4.21	3.35	2.96	2.73	2.57	2.46	2.37	2.31	2.20	2.13	1.93	1.67
28	4.20	3.34	2.95	2.71	2.56	2.45	2.36	2.29	2.19	2.12	1.91	1.65
29	4.18	3.33	2.93	2.70	2.55	2.43	2.35	2.28	2.18	2.10	1.90	1.64
30	4.17	3.32	2.92	2.69	2.53	2.42	2.33	2.27	2.16	2.09	1.89	1.62
32	4.15	3.29	2.90	2.67	2.51	2.40	2.31	2.24	2.14	2.07	1.86	1.59
34	4.13	3.28	2.88	2.65	2.49	2.38	2.29	2.23	2.12	2.05	1.84	1.57
36	4.11	3.26	2.87	2.63	2.48	2.36	2.28	2.21	2.11	2.03	1.82	1.55
38	4.10	3.24	2.85	2.62	2.46	2.35	2.26	2.19	2.09	2.02	1.81	1.53
40	4.08	3.23	2.84	2.61	2.45	2.34	2.25	2.18	2.08	2.00	1.79	1.51
60	4.00	3.15	2.76	2.53	2.37	2.25	2.17	2.10	1.99	1.92	1.70	1.39
120	3.92	3.07	2.68	2.45	2.29	2.18	2.09	2.02	1.91	1.83	1.61	1.25
∞	3.84	3.00	2.60	2.37	2.21	2.10	2.01	1.94	1.83	1.75	1.52	1.00

For copyright information see page i.

Critical values for the *F* test

0.1% points of the *F* distribution

v_2 \ v_1	1	2	3	4	5	6	7	8	10	12	24	∞
1	4053	5000	5404	5625	5764	5859	5929	5981	6056	6107	6235	6366
2	998.5	999.0	999.2	999.2	999.3	999.3	999.4	999.4	999.5	999.4	999.5	999.5
3	167.0	148.5	141.1	137.1	134.6	132.8	131.5	130.5	129.2	128.3	125.9	123.5
4	74.14	61.25	56.18	53.44	51.71	50.53	49.66	49.00	48.05	47.41	45.77	44.05
5	47.18	37.12	33.20	31.09	29.75	28.83	28.16	27.65	26.92	26.42	25.14	23.79
6	35.51	27.00	23.70	21.92	20.80	20.03	19.46	19.03	18.41	17.99	16.90	15.75
7	29.25	21.69	18.77	17.20	16.21	15.52	15.02	14.63	14.08	13.71	12.73	11.70
8	25.42	18.49	15.83	14.39	13.48	12.86	12.40	12.05	11.54	11.19	10.30	9.34
9	22.86	16.39	13.90	12.56	11.71	11.13	10.69	10.37	9.87	9.57	8.72	7.81
10	21.04	14.91	12.55	11.28	10.48	9.93	9.52	9.20	8.74	8.44	7.64	6.76
11	19.69	13.81	11.56	10.35	9.58	9.05	8.66	8.35	7.92	7.63	6.85	6.00
12	18.64	12.97	10.80	9.63	8.89	8.38	8.00	7.71	7.29	7.00	6.25	5.42
13	17.82	12.31	10.21	9.07	8.35	7.86	7.49	7.21	6.80	6.52	5.78	4.97
14	17.14	11.78	9.73	8.62	7.92	7.44	7.08	6.80	6.40	6.13	5.41	4.60
15	16.59	11.34	9.34	8.25	7.57	7.09	6.74	6.47	6.08	5.81	5.10	4.31
16	16.12	10.97	9.01	7.94	7.27	6.80	6.46	6.19	5.81	5.55	4.85	4.06
17	15.72	10.66	8.73	7.68	7.02	6.56	6.22	5.95	5.58	5.32	4.63	3.85
18	15.38	10.39	8.49	7.46	6.81	6.35	6.02	5.75	5.39	5.13	4.45	3.67
19	15.08	10.16	8.28	7.27	6.62	6.18	5.85	5.59	5.22	4.97	4.29	3.51
20	14.82	9.95	8.10	7.10	6.46	6.02	5.69	5.44	5.08	4.82	4.15	3.38
21	14.59	9.77	7.94	6.95	6.32	5.88	5.56	5.31	4.95	4.70	4.03	3.26
22	14.38	9.61	7.80	6.81	6.19	5.76	5.44	5.19	4.83	4.58	3.92	3.15
23	14.19	9.47	7.67	6.70	6.08	5.65	5.33	5.09	4.73	4.48	3.82	3.05
24	14.03	9.34	7.55	6.59	5.98	5.55	5.23	4.99	4.64	4.39	3.74	2.97
25	13.88	9.22	7.45	6.49	5.89	5.46	5.15	4.91	4.56	4.31	3.66	2.89
26	13.74	9.12	7.36	6.41	5.80	5.38	5.07	4.83	4.48	4.24	3.59	2.82
27	13.61	9.02	7.27	6.33	5.73	5.31	5.00	4.76	4.41	4.17	3.52	2.75
28	13.50	8.93	7.19	6.25	5.66	5.24	4.93	4.69	4.35	4.11	3.46	2.69
29	13.39	8.85	7.12	6.19	5.59	5.18	4.87	4.64	4.29	4.05	3.41	2.64
30	13.29	8.77	7.05	6.12	5.53	5.12	4.82	4.58	4.24	4.00	3.36	2.59
32	13.12	8.64	6.94	6.01	5.43	5.02	4.72	4.48	4.14	3.91	3.27	2.50
34	12.97	8.52	6.83	5.92	5.34	4.93	4.63	4.40	4.06	3.83	3.19	2.42
36	12.83	8.42	6.74	5.84	5.26	4.86	4.56	4.33	3.99	3.76	3.12	2.35
38	12.71	8.33	6.66	5.76	5.19	4.79	4.49	4.26	3.93	3.70	3.06	2.29
40	12.61	8.25	6.59	5.70	5.13	4.73	4.44	4.21	3.87	3.64	3.01	2.23
60	11.97	7.77	6.17	5.31	4.76	4.37	4.09	3.86	3.54	3.32	2.69	1.89
120	11.38	7.32	5.78	4.95	4.42	4.04	3.77	3.55	3.24	3.02	2.40	1.54
∞	10.83	6.91	5.42	4.62	4.10	3.74	3.47	3.27	2.96	2.74	2.13	1.00

1% points of the *F* distribution

v_2 \ v_1	1	2	3	4	5	6	7	8	10	12	24	∞
1	4052	5000	5403	5625	5764	5859	5928	5981	6056	6106	6235	6366
2	98.5	99.0	99.2	99.2	99.3	99.3	99.4	99.4	99.4	99.4	99.5	99.5
3	34.1	30.8	29.5	28.7	28.2	27.9	27.7	27.5	27.2	27.1	26.6	26.1
4	21.2	18.0	16.7	16.0	15.5	15.2	15.0	14.8	14.5	14.4	13.9	13.5
5	16.26	13.27	12.06	11.39	10.97	10.67	10.46	10.29	10.05	9.89	9.47	9.02
6	13.74	10.92	9.78	9.15	8.75	8.47	8.26	8.10	7.87	7.72	7.31	6.88
7	12.25	9.55	8.45	7.85	7.46	7.19	6.99	6.84	6.62	6.47	6.07	5.65
8	11.26	8.65	7.59	7.01	6.63	6.37	6.18	6.03	5.81	5.67	5.28	4.86
9	10.56	8.02	6.99	6.42	6.06	5.80	5.61	5.47	5.26	5.11	4.73	4.31
10	10.04	7.56	6.55	5.99	5.64	5.39	5.20	5.06	4.85	4.71	4.33	3.91
11	9.65	7.21	6.22	5.67	5.32	5.07	4.89	4.74	4.54	4.40	4.02	3.60
12	9.33	6.93	5.95	5.41	5.06	4.82	4.64	4.50	4.30	4.16	3.78	3.36
13	9.07	6.70	5.74	5.21	4.86	4.62	4.44	4.30	4.10	3.96	3.59	3.17
14	8.86	6.51	5.56	5.04	4.70	4.46	4.28	4.14	3.94	3.80	3.43	3.00
15	8.68	6.36	5.42	4.89	4.56	4.32	4.14	4.00	3.80	3.67	3.29	2.87
16	8.53	6.23	5.29	4.77	4.44	4.20	4.03	3.89	3.69	3.55	3.18	2.75
17	8.40	6.11	5.18	4.67	4.34	4.10	3.93	3.79	3.59	3.46	3.08	2.65
18	8.29	6.01	5.09	4.58	4.25	4.01	3.84	3.71	3.51	3.37	3.00	2.57
19	8.18	5.93	5.01	4.50	4.17	3.94	3.77	3.63	3.43	3.30	2.92	2.49
20	8.10	5.85	4.94	4.43	4.10	3.87	3.70	3.56	3.37	3.23	2.86	2.42
21	8.02	5.78	4.87	4.37	4.04	3.81	3.64	3.51	3.31	3.17	2.80	2.36
22	7.95	5.72	4.82	4.31	3.99	3.76	3.59	3.45	3.26	3.12	2.75	2.31
23	7.88	5.66	4.76	4.26	3.94	3.71	3.54	3.41	3.21	3.07	2.70	2.26
24	7.82	5.61	4.72	4.22	3.90	3.67	3.50	3.36	3.17	3.03	2.66	2.21
25	7.77	5.57	4.68	4.18	3.86	3.63	3.46	3.32	3.13	2.99	2.62	2.17
26	7.72	5.53	4.64	4.14	3.82	3.59	3.42	3.29	3.09	2.96	2.58	2.13
27	7.68	5.49	4.60	4.11	3.78	3.56	3.39	3.26	3.06	2.93	2.55	2.10
28	7.64	5.45	4.57	4.07	3.75	3.53	3.36	3.23	3.03	2.90	2.52	2.06
29	7.60	5.42	4.54	4.04	3.73	3.50	3.33	3.20	3.00	2.87	2.49	2.03
30	7.56	5.39	4.51	4.02	3.70	3.47	3.30	3.17	2.98	2.84	2.47	2.01
32	7.50	5.34	4.46	3.97	3.65	3.43	3.26	3.13	2.93	2.80	2.42	1.96
34	7.45	5.29	4.42	3.93	3.61	3.39	3.22	3.09	2.90	2.76	2.38	1.91
36	7.40	5.25	4.38	3.89	3.58	3.35	3.18	3.05	2.86	2.72	2.35	1.87
38	7.35	5.21	4.34	3.86	3.54	3.32	3.15	3.02	2.83	2.69	2.32	1.84
40	7.31	5.18	4.31	3.83	3.51	3.29	3.12	2.99	2.80	2.66	2.29	1.80
60	7.08	4.98	4.13	3.65	3.34	3.12	2.95	2.82	2.63	2.50	2.12	1.60
120	6.85	4.79	3.95	3.48	3.17	2.96	2.79	2.66	2.47	2.34	1.95	1.38
∞	6.63	4.61	3.78	3.32	3.02	2.80	2.64	2.51	2.32	2.18	1.79	1.00

For copyright information see page i.

Critical values for the Wilcoxon rank sum two-sample test

The critical values in these tables are for the Wilcoxon rank sum test statistic, W. Critical values for the Mann–Whitney test statistic, T, may be derived by subtracting $\frac{1}{2}m(m+1)$ (where m is the size of the sample from which the rank sum has been obtained). These values are tabulated on pages 72 and 73.

1-tailed →	5%	2½%	1%	½%
2-tailed →	10%	5%	2%	1%
m = 2, n				
5	3			
6	3			
7	3			
8	4	3		
9	4	3		
10	4	3		
11	4	3		
12	5	4		
13	5	4	3	
14	6	4	3	
15	6	4	3	
16	6	4	3	
17	6	5	3	
18	7	5	3	
19	7	5	4	3
20	7	5	4	3
21	8	6	4	3
22	8	6	4	3
23	8	6	4	3
24	9	6	5	3
25	9	7	5	3

1-tailed →	5%	2½%	1%	½%
2-tailed →	10%	5%	2%	1%
m = 3, n				
3	6			
4	6			
5	7	6		
6	8	7		
7	8	7	6	
8	9	8	6	
9	10	8	7	6
10	10	9	7	6
11	11	9	7	6
12	11	10	8	7
13	12	10	8	7
14	13	11	9	8
15	13	11	9	8
16	14	12	10	8
17	15	12	10	9
18	15	13	10	9
19	16	13	11	9
20	17	14	11	10
21	17	14	12	10
22	18	15	12	11
23	19	15	13	11
24	19	16	13	11
25	20	16	13	12

1-tailed →	5%	2½%	1%	½%
2-tailed →	10%	5%	2%	1%
m = 4, n				
4	11	10		
5	12	11	10	
6	13	12	11	10
7	14	13	11	10
8	15	14	12	11
9	16	14	13	11
10	17	15	13	12
11	18	16	14	12
12	19	17	15	13
13	20	18	15	13
14	21	19	16	14
15	22	20	17	15
16	24	21	17	15
17	25	21	18	16
18	26	22	19	16
19	27	23	19	17
20	28	24	20	18
21	29	25	21	18
22	30	26	21	19
23	31	27	22	19
24	32	27	23	20
25	33	28	23	20

1-tailed →	5%	2½%	1%	½%
2-tailed →	10%	5%	2%	1%
m = 5, n				
5	19	17	16	15
6	20	18	17	16
7	21	20	18	16
8	23	21	19	17
9	24	22	20	18
10	26	23	21	19
11	27	24	22	20
12	28	26	23	21
13	30	27	24	22
14	31	28	25	22
15	33	29	26	23
16	34	30	27	24
17	35	32	28	25
18	37	33	29	26
19	38	34	30	27
20	40	35	31	28
21	41	37	32	29
22	43	38	33	29
23	44	39	34	30
24	45	40	35	31
25	47	42	36	32

1-tailed →	5%	2½%	1%	½%
2-tailed →	10%	5%	2%	1%
m = 6, n				
6	28	26	24	23
7	29	27	25	24
8	31	29	27	25
9	33	31	28	26
10	35	32	29	27
11	37	34	30	28
12	38	35	32	30
13	40	37	33	31
14	42	38	34	32
15	44	40	36	33
16	46	42	37	34
17	47	43	39	36
18	49	45	40	37
19	51	46	41	38
20	53	48	43	39
21	55	50	44	40
22	57	51	45	42
23	58	53	47	43
24	60	54	48	44
25	62	56	50	45

1-tailed →	5%	2½%	1%	½%
2-tailed →	10%	5%	2%	1%
m = 7, n				
7	39	36	34	32
8	41	38	35	34
9	43	40	37	35
10	45	42	39	37
11	47	44	40	38
12	49	46	42	40
13	52	48	44	41
14	54	50	45	43
15	56	52	47	44
16	58	54	49	46
17	61	56	51	47
18	63	58	52	49
19	65	60	54	50
20	67	62	56	52
21	69	64	58	53
22	72	66	59	55
23	74	68	61	57
24	76	70	63	58
25	78	72	64	60

1-tailed →	5%	2½%	1%	½%
2-tailed →	10%	5%	2%	1%
m = 8, n				
8	51	49	45	43
9	54	51	47	45
10	56	53	49	47
11	59	55	51	49
12	62	58	53	51
13	64	60	56	53
14	67	62	58	54
15	69	65	60	56
16	72	67	62	58
17	75	70	64	60
18	77	72	66	62
19	80	74	68	64
20	83	77	70	66
21	85	79	72	68
22	88	81	74	70
23	90	84	76	71
24	93	86	78	73
25	96	89	81	75

1-tailed →	5%	2½%	1%	½%
2-tailed →	10%	5%	2%	1%
m = 9, n				
9	66	62	59	56
10	69	65	61	58
11	72	68	63	61
12	75	71	66	63
13	78	73	68	65
14	81	76	71	67
15	84	79	73	69
16	87	82	76	72
17	90	84	78	74
18	93	87	80	76
19	96	90	83	78
20	99	93	85	81
21	102	95	88	83
22	105	98	90	85
23	108	101	93	88
24	111	104	95	90
25	114	107	98	92

Critical values for the Wilcoxon rank sum two-sample test

1-tailed	5%	2½%	1%	½%
2-tailed	10%	5%	2%	1%
m n				
10 10	82	78	74	71
10 11	86	81	77	73
10 12	89	84	79	76
10 13	92	88	82	79
10 14	96	91	85	81
10 15	99	94	88	84
10 16	103	97	91	86
10 17	106	100	93	89
10 18	110	103	96	92
10 19	113	107	99	94
10 20	117	110	102	97
10 21	120	113	105	99
10 22	123	116	108	102
10 23	127	119	110	105
10 24	130	122	113	107
10 25	134	126	116	110
11 11	100	96	91	87
11 12	104	99	94	90
11 13	108	103	97	93
11 14	112	106	100	96
11 15	116	110	103	99
11 16	120	113	107	102
11 17	123	117	110	105
11 18	127	121	113	108
11 19	131	124	116	111
11 20	135	128	119	114
11 21	139	131	123	117
11 22	143	135	126	120
11 23	147	139	129	123
11 24	151	142	132	126
11 25	155	146	136	129

1-tailed	5%	2½%	1%	½%
2-tailed	10%	5%	2%	1%
m n				
12 12	120	115	109	105
12 13	125	119	113	109
12 14	129	123	116	112
12 15	133	127	120	115
12 16	138	131	124	119
12 17	142	135	127	122
12 18	146	139	131	125
12 19	150	143	134	129
12 20	155	147	138	132
12 21	159	151	142	136
12 22	163	155	145	139
12 23	168	159	149	142
12 24	172	163	153	146
12 25	176	167	156	149
13 13	142	136	130	125
13 14	147	141	134	129
13 15	152	145	138	133
13 16	156	150	142	136
13 17	161	154	146	140
13 18	166	158	150	144
13 19	171	163	154	148
13 20	175	167	158	151
13 21	180	171	162	155
13 22	185	176	166	159
13 23	189	180	170	163
13 24	194	185	174	166
13 25	199	189	178	170

1-tailed	5%	2½%	1%	½%
2-tailed	10%	5%	2%	1%
m n				
14 14	166	160	152	147
14 15	171	164	156	151
14 16	176	169	161	155
14 17	182	174	165	159
14 18	187	179	170	163
14 19	192	183	174	168
14 20	197	188	178	172
14 21	202	193	183	176
14 22	207	198	187	180
14 23	212	203	192	184
14 24	218	207	196	188
14 25	223	212	200	192
15 15	192	184	176	171
15 16	197	190	181	175
15 17	203	195	186	180
15 18	208	200	190	184
15 19	214	205	195	189
15 20	220	210	200	193
15 21	225	216	205	198
15 22	231	221	210	202
15 23	236	226	214	207
15 24	242	231	219	211
15 25	248	237	224	216
16 16	219	211	202	196
16 17	225	217	207	201
16 18	231	222	212	206

1-tailed	5%	2½%	1%	½%
2-tailed	10%	5%	2%	1%
m n				
16 19	237	228	218	210
16 20	243	234	223	215
16 21	249	239	228	220
16 22	255	245	233	225
16 23	261	251	238	230
16 24	267	256	244	235
16 25	273	262	249	240
17 17	249	240	230	223
17 18	255	246	235	228
17 19	262	252	241	234
17 20	268	258	246	239
17 21	274	264	252	244
17 22	281	270	258	249
17 23	287	276	263	255
17 24	294	282	269	260
17 25	300	288	275	265
18 18	280	270	259	252
18 19	287	277	265	258
18 20	294	283	271	263
18 21	301	290	277	269
18 22	307	296	283	275
18 23	314	303	289	280
18 24	321	309	295	286
18 25	328	316	301	292

1-tailed	5%	2½%	1%	½%
2-tailed	10%	5%	2%	1%
m n				
19 19	313	303	291	283
19 20	320	309	297	289
19 21	328	316	303	295
19 22	335	323	310	301
19 23	342	330	316	307
19 24	350	337	323	313
19 25	357	344	329	319
20 20	348	337	324	315
20 21	356	344	331	322
20 22	364	351	337	328
20 23	371	359	344	335
20 24	379	366	351	341
20 25	387	373	358	348
21 21	385	373	359	349
21 22	393	381	366	356
21 23	401	388	373	363
21 24	410	396	381	370
21 25	418	404	388	377
22 22	424	411	396	386
22 23	432	419	403	393
22 24	441	427	411	400
22 25	450	435	419	408
23 23	465	451	434	424
23 24	474	459	443	431
23 25	483	468	451	439
24 24	507	492	475	464
24 25	517	501	484	472
25 25	552	536	517	505

For larger values of m and n it is usually adequate to use a Normal approximation, with a continuity correction, with mean $\frac{1}{2}mn + \frac{1}{2}m(m+1)$ and variance $\frac{1}{12}mn(m+n+1)$.

Critical values for the Mann–Whitney test

The critical values in these tables are for the Mann–Whitney test statistic, T. Critical values for the Wilcoxon test statistic, W, may be derived by adding $\tfrac{1}{2}m(m + 1)$ (where m is the size of the sample from which the rank sum has been obtained). These values are tabulated on pages 70 and 71.

In the tables below the four significance columns give, for each pair (m, n), the critical value of T. The column headings are:

1-tailed	5%	2½%	1%	½%
2-tailed	**10%**	**5%**	**2%**	**1%**

(A dash — indicates no critical value exists at that level.)

m	n	5% / 10%	2½% / 5%	1% / 2%	½% / 1%
2	2	—	—	—	—
2	3	—	—	—	—
2	4	—	—	—	—
2	5	0	—	—	—
2	6	0	—	—	—
2	7	0	—	—	—
2	8	1	0	—	—
2	9	1	0	—	—
2	10	1	0	—	—
2	11	1	0	—	—
2	12	2	1	0	—
2	13	2	1	0	—
2	14	3	1	0	—
2	15	3	1	0	—
2	16	3	1	0	—
2	17	3	2	0	—
2	18	4	2	0	—
2	19	4	2	1	0
2	20	4	2	1	0
2	21	5	3	1	0
2	22	5	3	1	0
2	23	5	3	1	0
2	24	6	3	1	0
2	25	6	3	2	0
3	3	0	—	—	—
3	4	0	—	—	—
3	5	1	0	—	—
3	6	2	1	—	—
3	7	2	1	0	—
3	8	3	2	0	—
3	9	4	2	1	0
3	10	4	3	1	0
3	11	5	3	1	0
3	12	5	4	2	1
3	13	6	4	2	1
3	14	7	5	2	1
3	15	7	5	3	2
3	16	8	6	3	2
3	17	9	6	4	2
3	18	9	7	4	3
3	19	10	7	4	3
3	20	11	8	5	3
3	21	11	8	5	4
3	22	12	9	6	4
3	23	13	9	6	4
3	24	13	10	7	5
3	25	14	10	7	5
4	4	1	0	—	—
4	5	2	1	0	—
4	6	3	2	1	0
4	7	4	3	1	0
4	8	5	4	2	1
4	9	6	4	3	1
4	10	7	5	3	2
4	11	8	6	4	2
4	12	9	7	5	3
4	13	10	8	5	3
4	14	11	9	6	4
4	15	12	10	7	5
4	16	14	11	7	5
4	17	15	11	8	6
4	18	16	12	9	6
4	19	17	13	9	7
4	20	18	14	10	8
4	21	19	15	11	8
4	22	20	16	11	9
4	23	21	17	12	9
4	24	22	17	13	10
4	25	23	18	13	10
5	5	4	2	1	0
5	6	5	3	2	1
5	7	6	5	3	1
5	8	8	6	4	2
5	9	9	7	5	3
5	10	11	8	6	4
5	11	12	9	7	5
5	12	13	11	8	6
5	13	15	12	9	7
5	14	16	13	10	7
5	15	18	14	11	8
5	16	19	15	12	9
5	17	20	17	13	10
5	18	22	18	14	11
5	19	23	19	15	12
5	20	25	20	16	13
5	21	26	22	17	14
5	22	28	23	18	14
5	23	29	24	19	15
5	24	30	25	20	16
5	25	32	27	21	17
6	6	7	5	3	2
6	7	8	6	4	3
6	8	10	8	6	4
6	9	12	10	7	5
6	10	14	11	8	6
6	11	16	13	9	7
6	12	17	14	11	9
6	13	19	16	12	10
6	14	21	17	13	11
6	15	23	19	15	12
6	16	25	21	16	13
6	17	26	22	18	15
6	18	28	24	19	16
6	19	30	25	20	17
6	20	32	27	22	18
6	21	34	29	23	19
6	22	36	30	24	21
6	23	37	32	26	22
6	24	39	33	27	23
6	25	41	35	29	24
7	7	11	8	6	4
7	8	13	10	7	6
7	9	15	12	9	7
7	10	17	14	11	9
7	11	19	16	12	10
7	12	21	18	14	12
7	13	24	20	16	13
7	14	26	22	17	15
7	15	28	24	19	16
7	16	30	26	21	18
7	17	33	28	23	19
7	18	35	30	24	21
7	19	37	32	26	22
7	20	39	34	28	24
7	21	41	36	30	25
7	22	44	38	31	27
7	23	46	40	33	29
7	24	48	42	35	30
7	25	50	44	37	32
8	8	15	13	9	7
8	9	18	15	11	9
8	10	20	17	13	11
8	11	23	19	15	13
8	12	26	22	17	15
8	13	28	24	20	17
8	14	31	26	22	18
8	15	33	29	24	20
8	16	36	31	26	22
8	17	39	34	28	24
8	18	41	36	30	26
8	19	44	38	32	28
8	20	47	41	34	30
8	21	49	43	36	32
8	22	52	45	38	34
8	23	54	48	40	35
8	24	57	50	42	37
8	25	60	53	45	39
9	9	21	17	14	11
9	10	24	20	16	13
9	11	27	23	18	16
9	12	30	26	21	18
9	13	33	28	23	20
9	14	36	31	26	22
9	15	39	34	28	24
9	16	42	37	31	27
9	17	45	39	33	29
9	18	48	42	35	31
9	19	51	45	38	33
9	20	54	48	40	36
9	21	57	50	43	38
9	22	60	53	45	40
9	23	63	56	48	43
9	24	66	59	50	45
9	25	69	62	53	47

Critical values for the Mann–Whitney test

1-tailed	5%	2½%	1%	½%
2-tailed	10%	5%	2%	1%
m n				
10 10	27	23	19	16
10 11	31	26	22	18
10 12	34	29	24	21
10 13	37	33	27	24
10 14	41	36	30	26
10 15	44	39	33	29
10 16	48	42	36	31
10 17	51	45	38	34
10 18	55	48	41	37
10 19	58	52	44	39
10 20	62	55	47	42
10 21	65	58	50	44
10 22	68	61	53	47
10 23	72	64	55	50
10 24	75	67	58	52
10 25	79	71	61	55
11 11	34	30	25	21
11 12	38	33	28	24
11 13	42	37	31	27
11 14	46	40	34	30
11 15	50	44	37	33
11 16	54	47	41	36
11 17	57	51	44	39
11 18	61	55	47	42
11 19	65	58	50	45
11 20	69	62	53	48
11 21	73	65	57	51
11 22	77	69	60	54
11 23	81	73	63	57
11 24	85	76	66	60
11 25	89	80	70	63

1-tailed	5%	2½%	1%	½%
2-tailed	10%	5%	2%	1%
m n				
12 12	42	37	31	27
12 13	47	41	35	31
12 14	51	45	38	34
12 15	55	49	42	37
12 16	60	53	46	41
12 17	64	57	49	44
12 18	68	61	53	47
12 19	72	65	56	51
12 20	77	69	60	54
12 21	81	73	64	58
12 22	85	77	67	61
12 23	90	81	71	64
12 24	94	85	75	68
12 25	98	89	78	71
13 13	51	45	39	34
13 14	56	50	43	38
13 15	61	54	47	42
13 16	65	59	51	45
13 17	70	63	55	49
13 18	75	67	59	53
13 19	80	72	63	57
13 20	84	76	67	60
13 21	89	80	71	64
13 22	94	85	75	68
13 23	98	89	79	72
13 24	103	94	83	75
13 25	108	98	87	79

1-tailed	5%	2½%	1%	½%
2-tailed	10%	5%	2%	1%
m n				
14 14	61	55	47	42
14 15	66	59	51	46
14 16	71	64	56	50
14 17	77	69	60	54
14 18	82	74	65	58
14 19	87	78	69	63
14 20	92	83	73	67
14 21	97	88	78	71
14 22	102	93	82	75
14 23	107	98	87	79
14 24	113	102	91	83
14 25	118	107	95	87
15 15	72	64	56	51
15 16	77	70	61	55
15 17	83	75	66	60
15 18	88	80	70	64
15 19	94	85	75	69
15 20	100	90	80	73
15 21	105	96	85	78
15 22	111	101	90	82
15 23	116	106	94	87
15 24	122	111	99	91
15 25	128	117	104	96

1-tailed	5%	2½%	1%	½%
2-tailed	10%	5%	2%	1%
m n				
16 16	83	75	66	60
16 17	89	81	71	65
16 18	95	86	76	70
16 19	101	92	82	74
16 20	107	98	87	79
16 21	113	103	92	84
16 22	119	109	97	89
16 23	125	115	102	94
16 24	131	120	108	99
16 25	137	126	113	104
17 17	96	87	77	70
17 18	102	93	82	75
17 19	109	99	88	81
17 20	115	105	93	86
17 21	121	111	99	91
17 22	128	117	105	96
17 23	134	123	110	102
17 24	141	129	116	107
17 25	147	135	122	112
18 18	109	99	88	81
18 19	116	106	94	87
18 20	123	112	100	92
18 21	130	119	106	98
18 22	136	125	112	104
18 23	143	132	118	109
18 24	150	138	124	115
18 25	157	145	130	121

1-tailed	5%	2½%	1%	½%
2-tailed	10%	5%	2%	1%
m n				
19 19	123	113	101	93
19 20	130	119	107	99
19 21	138	126	113	105
19 22	145	133	120	111
19 23	152	140	126	117
19 24	160	147	133	123
19 25	167	154	139	129
20 20	138	127	114	105
20 21	146	134	121	112
20 22	154	141	127	118
20 23	161	149	134	125
20 24	169	156	141	131
20 25	177	163	148	138
21 21	154	142	128	118
21 22	162	150	135	125
21 23	170	157	142	132
21 24	179	165	150	139
21 25	187	173	157	146
22 22	171	158	143	133
22 23	179	166	150	140
22 24	188	174	158	147
22 25	197	182	166	155
23 23	189	175	158	148
23 24	198	183	167	155
23 25	207	192	175	163
24 24	207	192	175	164
24 25	217	201	184	172
25 25	227	211	192	180

For larger values of m and n it is usually adequate to use a Normal approximation, with a continuity correction, with mean $\frac{1}{2}mn$ and variance $\frac{1}{12}mn(m + n + 1)$.

Random numbers

68236	35335	71329	96803	24413
62385	36545	59305	59948	17232
64058	80195	30914	16664	50818
64822	68554	90952	64984	92295
17716	22164	05161	04412	59002
03928	22379	92325	79920	99070
11021	08533	83855	37723	77339
01830	68554	86787	90447	54796
36782	73208	93548	77405	58355
58158	45059	83980	40176	40737
91239	10532	27993	11516	61327
27073	98804	60544	12133	01422
81501	00633	62681	84319	03374
64374	26598	54466	94768	19144
29896	26739	30871	29795	13472
38996	72151	65746	16513	62796
73936	81751	00149	99126	23117
18795	93118	84105	18307	49807
76816	99822	92314	45035	43490
12091	60413	90467	42457	50490
41538	19059	69055	94355	84262
12909	04950	14986	08205	53582
49185	94608	87317	37725	66450
37771	48526	14939	32848	77677
22532	13814	69092	78342	37774
60132	24386	10989	54346	41531
23784	56693	45902	33406	53867
03081	20189	77226	89923	67301
51273	64049	19919	45518	43243
03281	40214	60679	68712	71636

Critical values for the Wilcoxon single-sample and paired-sample tests

1-tailed	5%	2½%	1%	½%
2-tailed	10%	5%	2%	1%
n				
2				
3				
4				
5	0			
6	2	0		
7	3	2	0	
8	5	3	1	0
9	8	5	3	1
10	10	8	5	3
11	13	10	7	5
12	17	13	9	7
13	21	17	12	9
14	25	21	15	12
15	30	25	19	15
16	35	29	23	19
17	41	34	27	23
18	47	40	32	27
19	53	46	37	32
20	60	52	43	37
21	67	58	49	42
22	75	65	55	48
23	83	73	62	54
24	91	81	69	61
25	100	89	76	68

1-tailed	5%	2½%	1%	½%
2-tailed	10%	5%	2%	1%
n				
26	110	98	84	75
27	119	107	92	83
28	130	116	101	91
29	140	126	110	100
30	151	137	120	109
31	163	147	130	118
32	175	159	140	128
33	187	170	151	138
34	200	182	162	148
35	213	195	173	159
36	227	208	185	171
37	241	221	198	182
38	256	235	211	194
39	271	249	224	207
40	286	264	238	220
41	302	279	252	233
42	319	294	266	247
43	336	310	281	261
44	353	327	296	276
45	371	343	312	291
46	389	361	328	307
47	407	378	345	322
48	426	396	362	339
49	446	415	379	355
50	466	434	397	373

For larger values of n, the Normal approximation with mean $\dfrac{n(n+1)}{4}$ and variance $\dfrac{n(n+1)(2n+1)}{24}$ should be used for $T = \min[P, Q]$.

1 Write down

The answer should be obvious and little or no calculation needed.

e.g. Write down the integral which should be calculated in order to find the area of the region between the curve and the x axis.

e.g. The roots of the cubic equation $x^3 - 5x^2 - 6x + 1 = 0$ are α, β and γ. Write down the values of $\alpha + \beta + \gamma$, $\alpha\beta + \beta\gamma + \gamma\alpha$ and $\alpha\beta\gamma$.

2 State

The answer is probably straightforward – if you understand what is being asked – with little or no work required.

e.g. State the condition under which the quadratic equation $z^2 + pz + q = 0$ does not have real roots, where p and q are real numbers.

3 Find

The answer is probably not quite so obvious and some work will be needed before you can give it. Any intermediate steps in your argument should be written down and included in your answer.

e.g. Find the co-ordinates of the points of intersection of the line $y = 2x$ with the curve $y = x^2 - 3x$.

4 Determine

Find precisely or define. The word 'determine' is rather stronger than 'find'.

e.g. Use calculus to find the co-ordinates of the turning points on this curve. Determine the nature of these turning points.

e.g. Determine whether or not your answer is correct to 3 decimal places.

5 Obtain

The word 'obtain' is used in much the same circumstances as 'determine'. It is somewhat stronger than 'find', usually implying that a degree of rigour is expected.

e.g. Obtain an expression for $\sum_{r=1}^{n} u_r$ where $u_r = 2^r + 4r$.

e.g. Hence obtain the best estimate you can of k, giving your answer to an appropriate number of significant figures.

6 Calculate

Some calculations (i.e. involving numbers) will be required and the answer will be a number, often given as a fraction or decimal.

e.g. Given that $y = x^3 - x + 6$ and P is $(-1, 6)$, calculate the value of $\frac{dy}{dx}$ at P.

7 Evaluate

Substitution in a formula or expression will be required, possibly after some initial work. Answers may be given in terms of functions such as $\ln 2$ or $\sin\frac{\pi}{10}$.

e.g. Evaluate the integral $\int_0^1 x\sqrt{1 + x^2}\,dx$

8 Exact

An exact answer is one where numbers are not given in rounded form. The answer will often contain an irrational number such as $\sqrt{3}$, e or π and these numbers should be given in that form. Do not use your calculator when you see the word 'exact'.

The use of the word 'exact' also tells you that rigorous (exact) working is expected in your answer to the question.

e.g. Find the exact solution of $\ln x = 2$.
The correct answer is e^2 and **not** 7.389056.

9 Show that

You are given a result and have to show that it is true. Because you are given the answer, the explanation has to be detailed and cover every step.

e.g. Show that the curve $y = x \ln x$ has a stationary point $\left(\frac{1}{e}, -\frac{1}{e}\right)$.

10 Explain

This is usually used when you are given a result and have to explain or interpret the reasoning behind it. As with 'show', the explanation has to be detailed and precise because you are given the answer.

e.g. Explain how, by using logarithms, the curve given by plotting y against x can be transformed into a straight line.

11 Prove

The use of the word 'prove' rather than 'show' indicates that a more formal statement of the argument is required, with careful logical justification for each step. It is often used for general results.

e.g. Given that $u_n = 2u_{n-1} + 8 - 4n$ for $n \geq 2$, $u_1 = 6$, prove, by induction or otherwise, that $u_n = 2^n + 4n$ for all positive integers n.

12 Deduce, Derive

These terms have the same meaning as 'prove' but are usually used in cases where the result is more limited (e.g. a special case) or the starting point is part of the way through a full proof. A rigorous argument is still required.

e.g. Deduce that if $y = mx + c$ is a tangent to the ellipse, then $c^2 = a^2 m^2 + b^2$.

13 Verify

This term is often used when you are required to show that a given result fits an equation. 'Verify' differs from 'show', in that you are allowed, and probably expected, to use the given result in your argument.

e.g. Verify that the tangent at Q passes through the point R(−4, −1).
(The tangent at Q was $y = x + 3$.)

e.g. Verify that the differential equation $\dfrac{dy}{dx} = x + y$ is satisfied by the family of curves $y = Ce^x - x - 1$.

In the case of a differential equation, if you are given initial conditions, they need to be checked as well, as part of the verification.

14 Hence

The next step must be based on what has gone before. Alternative methods should not be used.

e.g. You are given that $f(x) = 2x^3 - x^2 - 7x + 6$. Show that $f(1) = 0$. Hence find the three factors of $f(x)$.

15 Hence or otherwise

The next step may be based on what has gone before, but alternative methods are available and acceptable. If you choose 'hence', you may well already be some way towards the answer. The examiner will never suggest 'hence' if it is a poor method, but it may not be your preferred method.

e.g. Show that $(\cos x + \sin x)^2 = 1 + \sin 2x$ for all x.
Hence, or otherwise, find the derivative of $(\cos x + \sin x)^2$.

16 Expression

When one variable is written, algebraically, in terms of others, this is called an expression. An '=' sign is not part of the expression.

e.g. The first four terms in an infinite geometric progression are 54, 18, 6, 2.
Write down an expression for the nth term of the progression.

17 Formula

An expression for something. A formula is likely to be well known because it is often used, like that for the roots of a quadratic equation.

18. Express

Write in the form of an expression.

e.g. Express $2\cos x - 5\sin x$ in the form $r\cos(x + \alpha)$.

19 Plot

Mark points accurately, preferably on graph paper. You will either have been given the points or have had to calculate them. You will often then join them with a curve or a straight line, or draw a line of best fit through them.

e.g. Complete the table for $\log_{10} y$. Plot the points $(x, \log_{10} y)$ on the graph.

20 Sketch

Draw a diagram, not necessarily to scale and usually not on graph paper, showing the main features of a curve.

- Turning points
- Asymptotes
- Intersection with the y axis
- Intersection with the x axis
- Behaviour for large x ($+$ or $-$)

e.g. Sketch the curve with equation $y = \dfrac{x - 2}{(x - 1)(x - 3)}$.

21 Draw

Draw to an accuracy appropriate to the problem. You are being asked to make a sensible judgement about this.

e.g. Complete the table of values of $\log_{10} y$, and draw the graph of $\log_{10} x$ against $\log_{10} y$.

Modelling flowchart

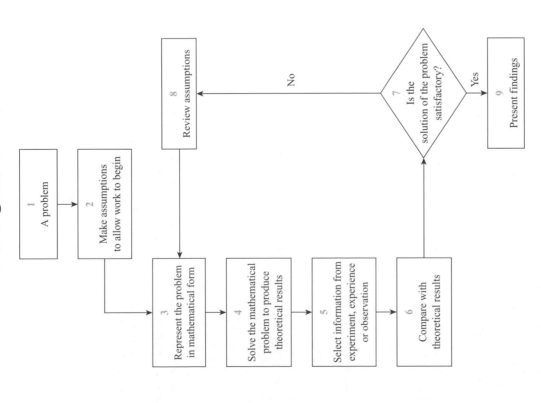

1 — A problem

2 — Make assumptions to allow work to begin

3 — Represent the problem in mathematical form

4 — Solve the mathematical problem to produce theoretical results

5 — Select information from experiment, experience or observation

6 — Compare with theoretical results

7 — Is the solution of the problem satisfactory?

8 — Review assumptions

9 — Present findings

No

Yes

Index

Index